D1286781

To Zack

All inquiries should be addressed to:
Barron's Educational Series, Inc.
250 Wireless Boulevard
Hauppauge, New York 11788

Library of Congress Catalog Card No. 91-38805

International Standard Book No. 0-8120-4772-9

Library of Congress Cataloging-in-Publication Data
Zweiback, Meg.
    Keys to parenting your one-year-old / Meg Zweiback.
        p.   cm. — (Barron's parenting keys)
    Includes index.
    ISBN 0-8120-4772-9
    1. Toddlers.   2. Child rearing.   3. Parenting.   I. Title.
    II. Series.
HQ774.5.Z84   1992
649'.122—dc20   91-38805
                                                          CIP

PRINTED IN THE UNITED STATES OF AMERICA

2345   5500   987654321

CONTENTS

INTRODUCTION

S ometime during the second year of your child's life, you will look at him and think: "I don't have a baby anymore!" You might be saddened at the thought, or delighted, or most likely both. This is the year when your baby changes into a toddler, a one-year-old who is no longer an infant but not quite a child, a person who is still very dependent on you for all of his needs but who is ready to break away from the shelter of your care to test his abilities in the world. His push for independence will mean that he pushes you away from him at times. His need for your love and care will mean that he will cling to you at other times. Your year together will be one of change, ambivalence, excitement, and sometimes frustration.

In this book, you will learn about the many ways your one-year-old will change this year. The first section, "How Your One-Year-Old Will Grow and Change," describes the ways your child develops in the way he thinks, the way he acts towards his parents, and the way he learns to use his senses and physical skills to learn. In this section, you also will find Keys about the developmental needs of one-year-olds in the daily life activities that take up so much of your time together: feeding, sleeping, toilet training, and discipline. Each Key in this section can be read separately, but your ability to understand your one-year-old's feelings and behavior will be enhanced if you read all of the Keys. The growth and development of a young child occurs in a jumble of leaps and bounds, steps forward and slides backward, and each area of development impacts on another. If you have an understanding of the overall progression you can expect during this year, it will be easier for you to observe, enjoy, and manage the ups and downs of your child's development.

The second section, "Temperamental Style," describes in detail the many ways in which children differ from one another in the way that they behave. All one-year-olds eventually will go through the same sequences of development, but each will do so in his own unique fashion. If you have an appreciation for your own child's style you will be much more comfortable with the ways in which he is different from other children, and perhaps the ways in which he is different from his parents.

The third section, "Typical Toddler Behavior and Misbehavior," describes all of the ways in which one-year-olds can challenge their parents' ability to be tolerant, loving, and patient. Although the typical toddler will give his parents hours of pleasure and joy, it is the moments that are less pleasurable and joyful that will make you feel as though you have a problem. In these Keys, you will learn how to manage, change, and live with your toddler as he tests his own limits and yours.

Part One

HOW YOUR
ONE-YEAR-OLD WILL
GROW AND CHANGE

When you look at a twelve-month-old, you see a baby. When you look at a twenty-four-month-old, you see a young child. Your one-year-old, throughout this year of her life, will be as amazed as you are at the sudden and rapid changes she makes as she grows. Your one-year-old will at times be so full of pride at her accomplishments that she will act as if you aren't around. At other times, she will be so overwhelmed by her efforts to be independent that she will cling to you like the baby she used to be.

Your one-year-old's development can be as exciting for you to watch as it is for her to experience. At the same time, you will be faced with challenges that you might not have expected. Your one-year-old's energy and drive may wear you out. Her emerging skills may frustrate you both when her slowness interferes with your need to move quickly. Her demands may make you doubt your ability to understand her needs. Above all, you may find that your pleasure in watching her grow is tinged with sorrow as you say good-bye to the soft intimacy of her infancy. Each step your child takes is one step away from you and her need for you. It is a challenge for parents of one-year-olds to help your child become independent without pulling her back too often or pushing her forward before she is ready.

1

THE SURGE FOR INDEPENDENCE

From the moment your baby was born, he depended on you to care for him. Without you there, he could not have survived. During his infancy, he learned that he could trust you to feed him, to hold him, to comfort him, and to entertain him. He was completely dependent on you, and as you cared for him he learned that the world was a safe place for him.

A baby sees his parents as an extension of himself, as a predictable part of his daily life. The trusting feelings that a well cared for baby develops towards his parents is called attachment, and as the baby becomes more attached to his parents, they in turn become attached to him. These bonds of caring, trust, and love endure over time and distance, and are the basis for your child's ability to have good feelings about himself and the world as he grows up.

As your baby grew older, he slowly realized that even though you had always seemed to be there when he needed you, you were not in fact always by his side. At these times he may have cried or called for you, anxiously and unhappily. You learned that by calling out to him when you were out of his sight, you could calm him. He learned that just because he couldn't see you, you were still in his world. Just as he learned by playing peek-a-boo that out of view does not mean gone, he learned, slowly, that his parents could leave him and not be gone forever.

Now, in your baby's second year, he has learned that the people he has come to love exist even when they are not with him. His memory for you makes it possible for him to hold on to you even when you are gone. He has the ability to leave your side without losing you. This mental image makes it possible for him to take advantage of his other emerging abilities to toddle away from you and explore the world without losing the safety of his home base.

His journey of exploration will not be an easy one. Your one-year-old constantly will be torn between the desire to leave you and to stay by your side, to let go and to hold on. You will see this internal battle every day as he struggles with his desire to be his own person while needing the security and love that his parents provide. Watch your toddler play when you are in a room with him. He may ignore your presence as he plays, seemingly independently. But if you leave, he may stop playing and follow you or howl for your return. He needs you to be with him so that he doesn't have to think about needing you!

The one-year-old is learning to be himself, and to establish that he is different from his parents. This need usually will blossom between fifteen and twenty-one months of age, although the timing is *extremely* variable. (Some toddlers don't get to this stage until they're almost three, but they do get there!) When your toddler begins to feel the need to separate from you, you will know it, because his way of letting you know will be to push you away from him in every way that he can! His favorite word often will seem to be "No!" He'll seem to have to do the opposite of what you want, and you'll have moments when you will feel that anything you do or say is wrong. Parents who have been used to a cooperative, delightful one-year-old often are knocked for a loop when their child reaches this stage, but they shouldn't be—

it's as normal and predictable an event as your child's learning to walk and talk.

It's hard when parents have to deal with a defiant one-year-old, but mothers often have a harder time than fathers. Because your toddler's negative behavior is his way of declaring his independence, he's likely to act more oppositional toward the person on whom he is most dependent for care. In most families, that person is the mother. After a day of doing battle with a toddler, a mother can feel especially incompetent if Dad comes home and seems to get nothing but cooperation and charm! Another variation of this pattern is seen in the child who spends his day with a sitter. As soon as his parents arrive, the child who has been an angel all day begins to act up, not because he's angry but because it is his parents he needs to react against.

Of course, your toddler will not be negative or defiant all of the time. He will express his desire to be independent by trying to do things himself and by imitating you or older children. As he takes pride in his achievements, you will see a look on his face that has been described as being in love with the world. Sometimes he will put so much energy into mastering one task that he will seem to lose ground in another area of his development. Parents often are perplexed when a toddler has had a wonderful afternoon of exploration and activity and then is clingy or tearful all the next day. Growth and change are exciting, but also stressful, and your toddler may take a leap forward one day but a step back the next.

Although the ups and downs of a one-year-old can be explained in terms of his need to become independent from his parents, most parents have trouble remembering the psychology of toddlerhood when they're trying to get through a difficult day! As parents, you can expect to feel challenged, and you shouldn't feel as though your job is to make your child feel happy at every moment. If you always try to please your one-year-old, he will push you further to get a reaction.

When their toddler is angry and negative, some parents get furious, perhaps even to the point of wanting to hurt their child. These feelings can be scary and overwhelming, but they're not unusual. If you find yourself reacting to your one-year-old in this way, your first step should be to protect him from your angry feelings. Put him in another room, count to ten slowly, and try to get calm. Call a friend, your partner, or a parents' hot line (see Suggested Reading and Resources, page 152). You won't be the first parent to need help with a one-year-old's negative behavior.

Even on the days when your one-year-old is delightful and mostly cooperative, you may feel a mixture of sad and happy feelings as you watch him growing up. Your toddler's independence is a loss for you, a farewell to a special time when he needed you and only you. At times, it may be hard for you to sort out *his* needs for *your* attention from *your* needs for *his* attention. You may find that you want to baby him more than he really needs, or to keep him close to you when he's trying to break away. Sometimes mothers and fathers disagree about how much time and attention a one-year-old still needs, each parent wanting the child to be as dependent or independent as the parent can handle at that moment. There isn't any right solution or timetable for helping a one-year-old to separate from his parents. Think of this year as your child's first tentative steps away from you, and your job as being the secure and supportive base from which he ventures forth. Watch your child, observe your reactions, and learn from your mistakes, and you will help him to gradually become himself.

7

2

HOW A ONE-YEAR-OLD THINKS

T hroughout this year your one-year-old will develop her ability to think, but it won't always be easy for you to figure out what is going on inside her mind. A toddler's way of thinking is so different from an adult's that most parents are never sure what their one-year-old understands and whether they are expecting too much or too little of her. The better you understand how your toddler learns to think, the better you can provide her with the support and stimulation she needs to develop her intelligence without putting pressure on her to perform beyond her capabilities.

If you watch your one-year-old as she plays, you will notice that she often looks serious and very involved in what she is doing, whether she is examining a toy car and rolling it across a tabletop, banging spoons, or fiddling with the knobs on your television set. A one-year-old is like a scientist who has to experiment before she can draw a conclusion. However, unlike the scientist who can learn from the experience of others, your one-year-old needs to learn from her own experience. In addition, because her memory is still short compared to that of an older child, she needs to do things over and over again to learn. Once she learns one thing, she often will repeat her experiment even more times, noticing small differences that an adult might not see. For example, a one-year-old might take a plastic toy and bang it on the coffee table. It makes an interesting sound, so she repeats the banging. She bangs harder and hears the change in sound. She might then take another toy and bang with that, noticing the difference in the sound and how it feels in her hand. After she has experimented with a few toys, she may pick up a plastic cup and bang some more. She may then take an object that is not a toy, and bang that. While she is banging, she is picking up cues from you about her behavior. You may not want her to bang at all, or you may let her bang toys but not cups, or you may let her bang plastic but not wood. You might ignore soft banging but stop her when she bangs loudly. From your toddler's point of view, every time she bangs, she learns something interesting, whether it is about the sound and feel of the objects she bangs or about the effect of her behavior on the people around her. No wonder a one-year-old keeps repeating what looks to you like the very same actions. To her, the actions are different and interesting each time.

If you recognize your one-year-old's need for repetitive experimentation, you will feel better about allowing her to choose what she wants to learn at a given moment. Your toddler may be in a room of interesting activities but want to spend all of her time in one corner with a single toy. Other children may move about more, but your child is learning just as effectively. A toddler does not need constant stimulation or dozens of toys and activities in order to develop her intelligence.

As you watch your toddler play, notice the look of satisfaction that you see on her face when she does something that pleases her. Her accomplishment may seem small, but if she feels as though she has mastered a problem, she will feel competent and good about herself. Those feelings will motivate her to want to work hard and learn more. Sometimes parents get in the habit of applauding or showing off their toddler's achievements. Their child may seem to perform better when she gets that response, because a parent's approval is a powerful motivator. However, some one-year-olds start showing off for parents rather than keep trying to learn new things that might interest them. A toddler can be trained by well-intentioned parents to value learning most when it is externally rewarded by applause and praise.

Parents often are amazed at what a toddler can remember. They also can be frustrated by her ability to forget one day what she seemed to remember the day before. The memory of a toddler increases daily, but it is still unpredictable. If you remind her of a rule every day, you will get her to cooperate, but she may need your reminders for weeks, months, or years. Even when she learns a rule, she will forget it if she is distracted or excited. Toddlers can't think ahead about what will happen next, so if they are tempted to break a rule they often will do so, forgetting that Mommy or Daddy scolded them the day before. However, parents can help toddlers to build their memory skills by having routines that are predictable and expectations that are consistent. Toddlers love structure, because it helps them to feel in control and to know what comes next.

A young one-year-old can watch you and copy what you do. As she gets older, she will be able to watch you and then to copy what you do after you have left the room. As she continues to watch, remember, and copy, she also will experiment with different ways of doing what she sees you do. As your toddler gets closer to two years old, she will be able to imitate a whole series of activities. She then will begin to combine the activities she has seen and imitated and use them to act like the person who does those things. She will be able to combine her direct experience with her mental pictures. This is called imaginary play, and when your one-year-old is closer to her second birthday, you will see more and more of this kind of pretending. That is why a young one-year-old would rather play with a real telephone or real pots and pans, whereas an older toddler will start to be interested in the bright plastic versions that fill the toy stores. It takes more imagination to play with the toys!

Although your one-year-old is learning to talk, and seems to understand many things that you say, she still learns primarily by real experience. She may listen attentively when you explain "why" or "how" to her, but her attention is mostly because she is interested in you, not because she can understand the content of what you are explaining. Some very bright one-year-olds seem to love parents' explanations and demonstrate a long attention span when parents take the time to talk to them. It's important to recognize that a one-year-old may enjoy and respond to parents' words but that they don't necessarily understand the concepts you discuss. When you talk to your child, notice if she seems eager or bored, curious or overloaded. It doesn't help your child if you are trying to teach her concepts that are beyond her.

When adults use words to explain concepts, they are using what we call symbolic thought. Words make it possible for us to share our understanding of the world without having to experience everything directly. A one-year-old can't think that way yet. She understands *only* what she can experience. Because she cannot draw conclusions beyond her experience, she sometimes makes connections between events that make sense to her but aren't correct. A toddler may learn that when she hears Daddy's car in the driveway, she then can expect Daddy to walk in the front door. If Daddy stops to talk to a neighbor instead of coming in the house right away, she may be confused or upset. If Daddy walks home one day, the toddler may not understand how he got home without driving up in the car. Explanations may soothe her, but it will be some time before she realizes that the sound of the car's engine and Daddy's arrival are not always connected.

When you appreciate your one-year-old's limited ability to make abstract connections, you also can begin to appreciate why she takes so much pleasure in learning in her own way. When she drops a toy, she is exploring the principle of gravity. When she tries to pull her wheeled cart across grass instead of cement, she is learning physics. When she learns that sugar and salt look alike but taste different, she is experimenting with chemistry and physiology. When she learns that some things she does please you and others do not, she is learning psychology! She needs you to provide her with an environment where she safely can explore and experiment in her own way and at her own pace, so that she can experience the joy of learning about the world. As you try to understand how she thinks, the more you will enjoy watching her learn.

3

LEARNING TO COMMUNICATE

Even though your one-year-old is just beginning to talk, he has been learning to communicate from the time he was born. Most of what he has learned you have taught him. He learned that when he cried, you would come to him and help him to get comfortable by feeding him or holding him. He learned that if he called you in a certain way, you would know that he was bored and needed attention. He learned that if he smiled and cooed, you would smile back and talk to him. Every time you responded to your baby you were teaching him about communication. Every time you and your baby exchanged sounds and words with each other you were teaching him language: the way human beings express and receive thoughts.

In this year of your child's life, he will greatly expand his understanding of the words you speak to him, his *receptive language skills*. He also will increase his ability to speak, his *expressive language skills*. His receptive language will advance more rapidly than his expressive language, and he will be able to understand much more than he can say. This gap between how much your child can understand and how little he is able to tell you is often a great frustration to a toddler. He knows what he wants, but he can't form the words to make his wants known to you. Tears and tantrums are common for the toddler who is frustrated by his inability to speak.

Children learn to speak at different rates, but there are typical milestones you should watch for as your child begins to talk.

By your child's first birthday, he will have a few words, probably labels for the most important people or objects in his life: "da," "ba," and "ma" are common first words. (A mother may feel bad if her baby doesn't say her name first. Often, a baby does not hear the word "Mommie" as much as he hears other words. Because babies learn to talk by imitating the sounds they hear, they may try to say "Daddy" or "bottle" first.)

Between your child's first and second birthdays, he gradually will learn to say 50 or more words (some understandable only to his own family) and to put together a few two-word sentences or questions. At the same time, he rapidly will be learning the meaning of your words. During this year of his life, he can learn to point to his body parts ("Where's your nose?"), to follow simple directions ("Throw the ball!"), to find pictures in a book ("Where's the kitty?"), and to respond to your questions ("Do you want a cookie?"). Even when he can't say words, he will have conversations with you and others by grunting, pointing, and showing you what he means.

As parents, you can help your child to communicate well with you and later with the world by stimulating his language development now. Most young children learn to talk without anyone seeming to teach them. That's because many of our responses to children come so naturally that we don't even realize how valuable they are. You probably set the stage for your child to talk when he was a baby. You talked to him in a high-pitched voice, you answered his gurgles as well as his cries, and you talked out loud about what you were

14

doing while your baby watched you. In all of these ways, you stimulated his language development.

During your child's second year, you can do even more to help his language skills. Research has shown that children who have parents and caregivers who talk to them frequently and directly have more advanced language skills when they reach preschool. Although some children learn to talk sooner and others later, parents can help the late bloomer by paying special attention to the way they talk to him. If your child already is saying many words, these techniques will assure that his language continues to develop rapidly.

- Have conversations with your child throughout the day. Talk about what you are doing. Use words to describe what you see him doing. "I'm stirring with the spoon. You have a spoon, too. You're banging with the spoon."
- When your child talks to you with sounds that are not yet words, respond to him as if he were talking. Let him learn that it is rewarding to try to speak, so that he will be motivated to keep trying. "Poo." "Oh, you want my spoon? Here, you take this. Is that what you want?"
- When your child uses single words, expand them into short sentences. "Baby?" "Yes, that is a baby. The baby is crying."
- As you talk, help your child to build his vocabulary by saying the names of things. One-year-olds learn best when they can see or touch an object, so talk about things that are within his sight or grasp. You can look at pictures in books together and talk about what he sees even if he isn't ready to listen to a story yet.
- Use simple rather than complex sentences. Although most one-year-olds will listen with pleasure while adults and older children talk, it can be hard for them to imitate what they hear if it is too complicated. A baby surrounded by a

constant buzz of conversation may take longer to learn to speak than the child who has a parent who also talks to him at his own level.

- Keep background noise, such as TV or radio, to a minimum. You may be able to screen out the conversation or music and listen to someone talking to you, but many young children can't.

- As your toddler begins to speak, respond to all of his words as if he were conversing in sentences. "Kit." "You see the kitty?" "Go." "Yes, the kitty goes through the door." "Kit?" "The kitty went outside. Do you want to see the kitty?" "Kit out?" "OK, let's go outside and see the kitty."

- Switch topics as often as you need to in order to keep a toddler's interest. His attention span is short. He may want to label what he sees in a garden and then stoop to examine the fine details of a rock. As he points, grunts, or attempts words, follow his lead.

- Ask your child questions, but don't worry if he doesn't answer. Pause, and then supply the words and response you would give him if he did speak. "What did you bring me?" "Oh, a doll!" "Thank you! Shall I put it here?" "No, not there? Over here? OK, that's where you want it."

- Sing songs or recite nursery rhymes. Toddlers love repetition. As your child gets older, pause at the end of lines to see if he wants to supply the last word. If he doesn't, say it yourself, until he gradually learns the game and begins to imitate you.

Sometimes parents are told that a child who is a late talker needs to be forced to speak. They may be told to make a child say a word rather than allowing him to point or grunt. They may be told not to respond to nonverbal attempts to communicate. However, if you don't respond to your child's first attempts at communication, he will become frustrated and angry and may even be less willing to talk. If you follow the techniques suggested above, you will be helping your child to develop his language skills, including speech, and to talk when he is ready.

Occasionally, a child may be late to talk for reasons other than being a late bloomer. The parent who observes the child at home is often the first person to notice that a child is not responding or vocalizing the same way as other children his age. A child who is not trying to talk and who is also not able to follow simple directions or respond to questions may not be hearing everything that others say to him. Even a fairly mild hearing loss, which can occur if a child has had frequent ear infections, can interfere with speech. Other risk factors for hearing loss are prematurity or illness at the time of birth. If any children in either parents' families have had difficulty with hearing, your child could have a problem as well. If you have any concerns about whether your child is hearing well, consult with your family doctor and ask that your child be evaluated by a professional audiologist who works with children. Although hearing loss can interfere with your child's learning to speak, early detection of a problem will assure that your child's overall language development does not suffer.

4

MOVING THROUGH SPACE

For most parents, the moment of their baby's first step is charged with excitement and meaning. Of all the many developmental achievements of a growing child, learning to walk independently is the one parents look forward to and remember the most. The child who is early to walk is hailed as precocious, and the child who takes his time may be a source of concern.

Even though the timing of your child's first step is emotionally significant to you, early or late walking does not influence your child's future accomplishments. A healthy child usually will begin to walk between nine and seventeen months of age. The typical twelve-month-old has learned to "cruise," that is, to walk while holding on to objects at shoulder height, such as a low table or the side of a chair. He may not be able to walk holding on to your hands if he has to raise his arms high to do so. He needs to be able to learn to develop a sense of balance and steadiness in his torso and legs, and most children will figure out the positions in which they feel most secure.

There is nothing that you can do to help your child to walk sooner than he is ready. The age your child walks is related to his internal maturation, not to environmental factors. Exercise or baby gym classes may be fun for parent and child, but the activities do not promote gross motor achievement. A child must be severely restricted in his experience before he will fail to learn to walk when he is ready. There is no justification for telling a parent whose child is late to walk that she should not hold him or spoil him by carrying him so much. A parent can, however, support his child's efforts to learn to walk in a way that builds continued self-confidence. As your child begins to pull himself to stand, to cruise, and to walk, you can provide him with a safe environment to explore, quiet encouragement, and a response that mirrors his own joy at his accomplishment.

As your child lets go of the furniture and begins the drunken looking, wide-based waddling gait that gives us the word-picture of a toddler, you will see his face glow with enthusiasm. You also may see him persist in his efforts to master his new skill far beyond his physical endurance. The newly walking one-year-old may be unwilling to sleep, to eat, or to play with favorite toys if it means giving up practice time. He may seem fragile in mood, obsessed with his quest for competence. As his skills improve, so will his temper.

As a parent, you can learn a great deal from your child by watching his style as he learns to walk. Is he cautious or reckless? Does he seem propelled by his motor skills or does he look for a destination before he gets going? When he falls, does he need comfort or does he persist without a whimper? When he gets stuck does he try to figure out what to do on his own or does he look to you for help? Are you able to give him the time and encouragement to solve the problem on his own or do you leap in to fix things for him? Whatever you observe, try to remember that if you can let your child learn in his own way and at his own pace, his inner motivation will be enough to make him successful.

Once your child is walking, you will find that he sees his world differently. He can now move about in space, questing after excitement and seeing the world from a new perspective. He can move away from you quickly and efficiently, fueling his drive for independence. At the same time, the distance he creates can be terrifying for him, and it is not unusual to see a one-year-old who has toddled away from his mother crying pitifully for her to come after him.

As your child gets the balance and control to be able to walk, he also will be learning to run and climb. All of these new motor accomplishments create threats to his safety. He needs to be restrained when you are near the street or in a parking lot and must learn to hold your hand whenever you tell him to. You will have to go through your home again to childproof cupboards, drawers, bookcases, and tabletops. A one-year-old can push a chair to a kitchen counter to climb up and play with the microwave, or vault to the top of the bathroom sink to investigate the medicine cabinet. No matter how carefully you childproof, however, your toddler's speed and curiosity will drive him into danger you can't predict. It is never safe to leave a one-year-old unsupervised, and as any experienced parent can tell you, if your child is out of your sight and you can't hear him, he's probably in trouble!

As you begin to think of your child as a walker you may feel that he needs special shoes to support his toddling about. He doesn't. The best shoes for a one-year-old are soft soled with enough support to protect the foot from injury and room enough for toes to grow. Shoes with high ankle support and stiff soles will not help the child to walk and may even encourage falls. Your newly walking child will tumble and fall, no matter what, and it is the supportive parent rather than the supportive shoe that will help him to eventually learn to move with skill and speed.

5

MANIPULATING THE ENVIRONMENT

Your one-year-old always is learning, and one way she learns is by touching, feeling, moving, and manipulating the objects in her environment. If you want to see a busy mind at work, set your toddler on the floor of your kitchen and give her some wooden spoons, some unbreakable dishes, and a plastic bowl filled with some of her own toys. Your child will happily mess with her array of equipment, exploring the many ways the objects can be arranged and rearranged.

Your toddler's ability to learn is enhanced by her increased competence in using her hands and wrists as she develops her *fine motor skills* during the second year of life. As she puts her toys in and out of a container, as she bangs and throws her blocks and balls, as she makes towers that stand or tumble, she is experimenting with the physical properties of her world. Hard and soft, big and small, full and empty, are concepts that your child figures out through her fine motor play. She also learns from your attitudes towards her play. If she hears too many "no's" or finds that everything she wants to touch is off limits, she may begin to feel that her curiosity and exploration is not acceptable to you. If you encourage her activities by providing her with safe and stimulating objects to manipulate, you also will be encouraging her love for learning. As an added benefit, you will find that her playtime gradually will increase and you will have a few more minutes to yourself!

Throughout the year, you will notice that your child becomes more skilled in the way she handles small objects. One of the best toys you can get for your one-year-old is a set of 1½" square blocks, painted with nontoxic colors. The younger one-year-old will be able to stack two blocks, transfer them hand to hand (often storing an extra one in her mouth), and will be delighted to fill and empty a bucket with blocks, over and over again. In these simple activities, you can see some of the important characteristics of the one-year-old's fine motor development.

She has the visual and perceptive ability to balance one block on another, although she might not think of doing so unless you show her. She uses her mouth as a sensory organ, so most toys and other objects will be tasted or chewed as she plays with them. Parents of one-year-olds get annoyed when their child "puts everything in her mouth," but that is what normal toddlers are supposed to do. (It's not surprising that when toddlers play together and pass toys back and forth this mouthing behavior results in spreading colds and other illnesses among them.) The emptying of containers is a common toddler activity, and she will be endlessly delighted to take the blocks out of a bowl, the socks out of your drawers, or all of your paraphernalia out of your purse. If you put things back, she will empty them again, pleased that you like the activity as much as she does!

As your child matures and she begins to coordinate her hand movements with the way she sees, you can give her a box with a hole cut in its lid slightly larger than the blocks. She will try to put the blocks through the hole and be delighted to see them disappear. If you get her a simple shape sorter box with different shapes of plastic blocks and a lid cut to match the shapes, she will experiment over and over again with turning the shapes until they fit, although it will take her many months before she figures out which shapes match. If you mix her small wooden blocks in with the larger shapes she'll be able to fit them through all of the openings and feel successful as she is mastering the more difficult shapes.

As your toddler matures in the way she thinks, she will begin to arrange her blocks and other toys in ways that reflect her increased cognitive skills. She may line the blocks up, or use them to symbolize a house or a piece of furniture for a doll. Using an object to carry out an imaginative idea is a very important developmental achievement that will occur as she gets closer to two years of age.

At the same time your toddler develops her imagination, she also develops her curiosity about the way objects are made. The younger one-year-old will take a new toy and feel it, turn it, bang it, or taste it. The older one-year-old continues her investigation by using her coordinated thumb, finger, and wrist movements to manipulate the toy and even to try to take it apart! The younger toddler will enjoy the simple challenge of pushing buttons and flipping light switches, but the older child will discover how to turn knobs and unlock doors.

As your one-year-old grows, she will try to do what she sees you doing. You can build on your toddler's desire to imitate you by letting her feed herself with her fingers and a spoon and to drink from a cup. The older toddler can learn to brush her teeth (you'll have to finish the job), take off her clothes, comb her hair, and wash and dry her hands. Don't worry if she is messy or clumsy in her attempts. All of the complicated hand movements that these tasks require will emerge without your teaching, but the more opportunities you offer for practice the more coordinated she will become.

As your toddler's memory improves, you will see her imitating behavior she saw you do only once, sometimes leaving out a step, but trying valiantly to reconstruct her observations.

Toddlers also want to imitate their parents' writing with pens and pencils, but they'll find it easier to hold a fat crayon. A one-year-old can hold a crayon, but her arm movements are too large and circular for her to be able to keep her drawings on a small sheet of paper. Give her big pieces of inexpensive paper to work with, on the floor, on a table, or tacked to the wall. Most toddlers will happily color in books or on walls if you don't keep an eye on them, so keep the crayons and your own instruments stored out of reach. Many parents have gone looking for the suddenly silent toddler and found her busy redecorating the wallpaper in the living room!

Your toddler's increased fine motor skills will make it necessary for you to childproof your home beyond the steps you took during her first year of life. Because one-year-olds can be expected to put anything and everything in their mouths, choking and poisoning become greater dangers. Their ability to stand, reach, and climb means that simply storing potential hazards out of reach may not be enough. Dangerous objects must be stored out of sight and safeguarded with safety shields and locks. The pennies in your bureau drawer or the vitamins in your medicine cabinet can go from your toddler's hand to her mouth without your noticing, so install the special hooks that keep drawers and cabinets from opening fully. Even if you try to teach your toddler not to touch or taste, her drive to explore and experiment will outweigh her ability to remember rules. You must protect her from temptation.

6

~~~~~~

FEEDING

The physical, developmental, and emotional changes that occur in the twelve- to twenty-four-month-old toddler can make feeding and mealtimes a challenge for any parent. Many parents are unsure how to respond to the changes in appetite and eating patterns that can be expected during the second year of life. The baby who could be counted on to respond eagerly to being fed often becomes a toddler who is a reluctant and resistant eater. The satisfying feeling you may have experienced from watching your baby eat enthusiastically may be lost as you see his appetite become irregular and unpredictable. If you try to make your growing child eat like a baby, he will rebel, actively by pushing food away, or quietly by refusing to eat. Because you'll be offering your toddler food several times a day, the patterns you create now will be very important as he develops his attitudes about eating. What your child learns as a toddler about eating will influence how he eats as an older child and as an adult.

As you plan for the nutritional needs of your toddler, it may help to think about how different he is now from when he was a little baby. As an infant, your child needed to be fed very frequently. His stomach size was quite small, so he filled up quickly, but he was growing so rapidly that he needed to eat again before long. During your child's first year of life, he probably tripled his birth weight and grew nine inches in length! Your toddler, during his second year, will only gain half the weight and add half the height he did during his first year. He can eat more at one time, and his digestive system is more mature, allowing him to get more nutritive value out of his food. He won't need to eat as often as he did as a baby, and the overall quantity of food he eats may decrease as well.

Your toddler also is going to want to be an active participant in feeding himself, unlike the cooperative baby who opened his mouth every time you offered him a spoon. Your child's need to use his hands and master the fine motor coordination of his small muscles makes him want to feed himself, usually with his fingers but sometimes with a spoon. Even if he is very hungry, he may prefer to eat the tiny bits that he can get to his mouth on his own to the larger spoonfuls you offer. If you give him time to feel as though he's getting to feed himself by placing small bits of finger foods in front of him, he may allow you to occasionally offer him a spoonful of another food while he stays busy. You may find that if you stay casually interested and helpful, your toddler will enjoy having you help him feed himself in the same way he lets you play with him and his toys.

Staying casually involved is particularly important as your one-year-old begins to assert himself as an independent and separate person. When he was a baby, he was completely dependent on you to recognize his hunger, provide him with milk and food, and to control all of his feeding. That dependent, needy baby now wants to become an independent, resourceful child, and pushing you away as you try to help him eat is a way of saying, "I want to take care of myself." Of course, your toddler can't really take care of himself, but he can tell you he wants to by refusing to be fed and resisting your cajoling him to eat. Once your toddler begins to assert his independence, you can be sure that any pressure you put on him to eat will be met with rejection.

Parents may find that this rejection makes them feel hurt or even angry. It's not just that your child doesn't want to eat—it's that the loving, pleasant time you enjoyed with your baby has been replaced with a battle. Some parents find it very hard to give up control of feeding time. They will cajole or pressure their child with games or even force him to take a few more bites. The parent may feel that it's important for the child's nutritional needs to make him eat, but even a temporary victory by the parent will backfire. Your toddler's needs to feel independent and self-reliant are really too strong to ignore, and the child who seems to give in may wind up with eating problems later in life.

Parents can make an independent toddler a better eater by providing nutritious food at regular times, usually in small meals and snacks five to six times a day. Offer the food in a form that your toddler can accept easily. Have a special place for your child to sit, in a high chair or a booster seat at the table. Offer him small amounts of bite-sized food on a small, unbreakable plate with a raised edge to push food against. Give him a child-size spoon and fork to practice with. Give him a half inch of milk in a clear plastic cup so that he can sip without spilling much. Notice the textures and thickness of food that your child finds most appealing. Don't assume that your child doesn't like a food because he rejects it once. Some children need repeated exposures to a dab of a new food before they'll try it.

Remember that toddlers can choke on foods that are bigger than bite size, so even soft food should be cut small. Round foods, such as hot dogs or grapes, should be cut in quarters. Hard foods that need careful chewing, such as carrot sticks, popcorn, or peanuts, can be accidentally inhaled into the lungs rather than swallowed, so these foods should be avoided until your child is three years old and can grind up food with his back molars.

Keep the mealtime pace slow, but don't allow your child to mix up playtime with mealtime. If your child throws his food or dishes on the floor, don't pick them up. Take his action as his signal that he's all done and remove him from the table calmly, even if he's hardly eaten. After you respond this way a few times, he'll realize that his behavior doesn't get a rise from you, and he'll stop throwing food until he's really finished eating!

Many adults enjoy the dinner meal as a time to talk and relax while they eat. When you have a toddler, you may find that his idea of meals is different from yours. Although some one-year-olds can enjoy playing with their mashed potatoes for a long period, many see feeding time as nothing more than fueling time and will not be willing to sit still while parents are talking to each other. You'll have to decide whether you want to keep your attention on your toddler while you eat or plan a later meal for yourselves to enjoy alone. This phase of your child's life is temporary and you can look forward to family mealtimes in a few years when he is old enough to understand and participate in conversation.

In order to plan for feeding your one-year-old, you'll need to know the types and amounts of food he needs for good nutrition. These guidelines will help you plan the meals and snacks he needs daily. Parents sometimes are surprised at the small amount of food a toddler really needs to grow well and be healthy.

Milk   16–24 ounces a day. If your one-year-old is a picky eater, limit milk to 16 ounces a day.

Fruits   2 servings a day of 2 tablespoons each serving, *plus* 3 ounces orange juice or a vitamin C source. If your one-year-old drinks more than 4 ounces of juice a day and doesn't want to eat much, he probably is substituting juice for other foods.

Vegetables   3 servings a day of 2 tablespoons each serving.

Grains   6 servings a day: serving size is about ½ ounce, for example, ½ slice bread, 2 tablespoons rice or pasta.

Protein   2 servings a day: serving size is 1 ounce meat or legumes, 1 egg, or 1 tablespoon peanut butter. Include an iron source: meat, legumes, iron fortified cereal.

Source: Adapted from the United States Department of Agriculture's *Food Guidelines*, revised in November 1990.

Toddlers usually don't need vitamins, but if your child consistently eats less than the recommended portions of each of these food groups, a multivitamin drop with added iron will protect him. If he refuses all milk products, he might need a calcium supplement. If he doesn't drink water, or if you live in an area without a fluoridated water supply, he should receive a fluoride supplement. Your health care provider can tell you the type and amount of extra vitamins or minerals your child needs.

Although feeding a toddler can be a challenge, it's important to remember that your one-year-old's behavior at mealtime is just another part of this stage of development. The more that you can relax and enjoy his desire for independence and self-control, the easier your feeding relationship will be with your child.

7

SLEEP

After your child becomes a one-year-old you will see him become increasingly regular in his sleep patterns. When your child turns one, he probably will be sleeping 13 to 14 hours out of every 24. The typical one-year-old sleeps 10 to 11 hours during the night and then takes two naps, the first beginning about two hours after he wakes up in the morning and the second in the afternoon. At some time during this year, he may begin to stay awake through the morning and to take one long nap at midday. By his second birthday, his overall need for sleep will be about the same or slightly less, but he probably will take a nap for one to three hours in the early afternoon. These figures are average and some children need more or less sleep than others. However, children who don't get enough sleep often act crabby or fussy rather than tired, so if you have a child who seems to need less sleep but is often in a bad mood, you may need to look at his sleep habits.

In order for your child to get enough sleep and to develop good sleep patterns, you will have to plan evening routines that help him to relax and get ready for bed. Children sleep better when they have a regular bedtime that doesn't vary too much from day to day. Choose a bedtime that works for you and your child. Parents who work away from home during the day often want their child to stay up later than parents who can see their child during the day. However, a child who is kept up *too* late often will become more keyed up and excitable from fatigue, so pay attention to your child's cues. If he rubs his eyes or begins to get droopy, he's ready for sleep, even if he seems to get a second wind.

Try to begin getting your child ready for bed about a half hour before you want him settled. Toddlers like routines because they feel comfortable and secure when they know what will happen next. If both parents participate in the bedtime routine, a toddler can adjust to slightly different patterns from each, but the overall routine should not change dramatically. Bedtime routines can include bathing, changing into pajamas and a fresh diaper, brushing teeth, and some cozy parent time. Exciting games and wrestling matches are a wonderful way to play with your child, but most toddlers will find it difficult to fall asleep if these activities take place right before it's time to go to sleep. Story telling, reading, and singing are nice, soothing ways to end the day. If your child has a special blanket or transitional object to hold onto, he may find it very comforting at this time. Many parents will say good night with a ritual, such as each parent coming in for a hug and kiss or saying a special good night to the stuffed animals and toys. Most children will prefer to have a dim light or night light on. If you shade the windows, you may be able to keep out early morning light and noise and help your child to sleep later.

Some one-year-olds have difficulty falling asleep at night. Parents may find that their child wants them to stay with him until he is fast asleep. Some parents find that their child needs to be rocked or nursed or held before he will fall asleep. One-year-olds don't like to be left alone, day or night, so it isn't surprising that they protest when a parent tries to say good night at the end of the day. However, some children have more difficulty with sleep than others because in addition to the normal desire to have a parent stay with them, they also have developed the habit of needing the parent's help to fall asleep. Everyone has habits that help them to fall asleep. For example, most adults think it is necessary to fall asleep in a darkened room with a pillow under their heads . If you asked them to fall asleep lying flat with the lights on, they would be very upset and would have a hard time relaxing. In the same way, a young child may get used to having a parent there to help him fall asleep. If the parent leaves him alone, he protests. If your child has this kind of habit and you want to change it, try to withdraw gradually from your child's side. Instead of holding him, sit in a chair by the crib for a few nights, telling him calmly that you are there but that he must fall asleep on his own. After he can handle this separation, begin to move away from the crib. Eventually, you can move your chair outside the door and your child will have developed the habit of falling asleep on his own.

Many children wake during the night and call out or cry for their parents. If your child calls you during the night, he needs you. If you think that he is wet, or hungry, or in pain, you will need to help him with his problem before you and he can go back to sleep. However, some children who wake during the night don't seem to need anything but the parent's arrival. They go back to sleep as soon as the parent holds them or rocks them. Unfortunately, these children keep waking up, often several times every night. Parents become increasingly exhausted and often angry as well. If your child wakes up during the night and seems to need you to help him return to sleep, the cause is almost always a *sleep association habit*. Your child has learned to put himself to sleep with your help, and he doesn't know how to go to sleep without you. He probably needs your help at bedtime as well. During his deep sleep phases, he stays asleep. But when he gets to a lighter stage of sleep during the night and discovers that you aren't there, he calls to you. (A variation of this problem is seen in the child who goes to sleep sucking a pacifier. When he awakens during the night and can't find it, he calls out to his parent to help. Once the pacifier is in his mouth he goes right back to sleep.) If your child seems to have a habit like this, the time to help him learn to fall asleep on his own is at bedtime. Gradually remove yourself from assisting him to fall asleep. Once he can fall asleep at bedtime on his own, he will be able to return himself to sleep during the night as well.

If your child wakes you up during the night with crying and appears fearful and clingy when you go to him, he probably is waking up from a *nightmare* or a bad dream. A one-year-old can't talk well enough to be able to tell you about his dream, but you will be able to see by his tearful reaction that something has happened that is troubling him. We don't know for sure what a one-year-old dreams about, but because many of a toddler's fears are related to separation from his parents, it is likely that he is having a dream about not being able to get to Mommy or Daddy. When you arrive, he will be relieved but still upset, and he may not want you to leave him. It is reasonable to stay with him until he falls back asleep or to bring him into bed with you. Nightmares sometimes occur when a child is experiencing stress in daily life, such as starting child care, moving to a new house, or going on vacation. If your child is having frequent nightmares that continue for several weeks, it's important to examine his daytime life to see if he is having ongoing stress that may be troubling him during the night.

Another cause of night waking in a toddler is a *night terror*. If your child is having a night terror, you will hear him crying and perhaps thrashing about. When you go to him, he will be crying hard and looking very upset. His eyes will look glazed and he will not seem to see you. Unlike the child who has had a nightmare, the child who is having a night terror will not reach out to you or want comfort. That is because a child who is having a night terror actually is still asleep and the child is not aware that he is crying or that you are there. Night terrors are very frightening to parents, but do not trouble children because they don't remember them. In fact, the most difficult part of a night terror is resisting the urge to wake your child. If you wake him and he sees your worried faces, he may be frightened. If you just stay with him until he returns to quiet sleep or awakens on his own, he will be fine. Night terrors, like nightmares, are very normal and may result from a change in your child's daily life. If they occur frequently, it can be helpful to look for a source of continuing stress during your child's day.

If your child sleeps well, your life as a parent will be much easier. When your child doesn't get enough sleep, he may be cranky and difficult. When you don't get enough sleep, you may be irritable and impatient. It's worth the effort to help your child learn to sleep at night so that you can be a better parent during the day.

8

TOILET TRAINING READINESS

I f you've talked about toilet training to parents whose toddlers are now grown, you may have heard that they began training as soon as their children could walk. However, in the past 20 years, ideas about toilet training have changed, for many good reasons. As we have learned more about child development, we've seen that children whose parents observe them and wait for signs of readiness before beginning training learn to use the toilet more easily and with fewer struggles than in the past.

Pediatrician T. Berry Brazelton, in a study of over a thousand young children, found that with a *child centered* approach to toilet training, most children are trained by twenty-eight months of age, and virtually all are trained by three years. Brazelton's study also showed that there is a wide variation in the age of toilet training, and that early toilet training is not a sign of a child's intelligence or a parent's competence.

Sometime during your child's second year of life you will probably see the signs of readiness for toilet training. Your toddler will first learn to recognize the feeling he has *after* he has urinated or had a bowel movement. Then he will learn what it feels like at the time he is doing so. Last, after many months, he will recognize the feelings he has when he is *ready* to go. Keep in mind that you may not see these signs until late in this year or even after his second birthday.

Your child is ready for you to begin the first steps of toilet training him when you see these signs:

- Your toddler lets you know by his facial expression, gestures, or words that he wants to be changed into a clean diaper. You can help him get to this stage by making diaper changing a pleasant time, saying "Doesn't that feel nice?" when he's clean. Most children under the age of eighteen months don't feel or pay attention when they're passing urine or a bowel movement, so don't expect to see this behavior in a young one-year-old.

Don't frown or complain about the mess in your child's diapers. He'll think you are disapproving of *him* and he won't understand. However, you *can* praise him when he tells you he needs to be changed because then you are rewarding him for taking care of himself.

- Your toddler is imitating lots of adult behavior, such as wanting to brush his teeth, use a fork, or sweep the kitchen. He may not want you to help him with these activities.

These are examples of his inner drive to be competent. If you praise him for his efforts, even if they make more work for you at first, you'll be boosting his pride in doing things for himself. This pride becomes a strong motivation for his desire to be toilet trained.

- Your toddler can understand and follow simple directions and has enough vocabulary to tell you when he needs to go. Teach him words that you are comfortable using and that he can pronounce: "Pee, poop, and potty" are popular choices.
- Your toddler is able to sit still on a small chair for three to five minutes while you read or talk to him. Many children

can't sit still this long until they have been walking and running well for several months. *Never* force your child to stay sitting on a potty chair or toilet.

- Your toddler is not in an intense phase of rebelliousness or negativity. Although one-year-olds are negative and oppositional as part of their normal development, most toddlers will go through periods when they seem to be battling their parents even more than usual. If you introduce toilet training at this point, your efforts probably will make life miserable for you and your child.

Once you observe these signs of readiness, provide your child with a small potty chair. Most children do best with a simple small chair with a toilet-like seat. They are most comfortable when they can sit straight with their feet on the ground. You can let your child practice using the chair with his clothes on for a few days, and then have him get used to sitting on it with a bare bottom. It's a good idea to keep the chair in the bathroom rather than having it in his room, so that you are encouraging him to be more grown-up. Little boys may want to stand up to urinate like Daddy, and you can provide a step in front of the big toilet to help.

Dress your child in clothing that he can remove himself, choosing pants with elastic waistbands rather than buttons and avoiding overalls that require your assistance. Plan for a few regular times every day to have your child sit on the potty for two to three minutes while you talk to him or read him a short story. Try to choose times when you've noticed he's wet or had a bowel movement. Usual times for most children are when they awaken in the morning, after meals and snacks, after naps, and at bathtime.

If your child goes in the potty, tell him that he's done a good job, but don't heap on the praise too heavily. Take the contents of the pot and tell him you are going to put it in the toilet. Tell him that you are going to flush his pee or poop just like you flush your own. You can ask him if he wants to watch, and whether he wants to flush the toilet himself. Some toddlers are very interested in watching things go down the toilet. If your child is, be sure to let him know that the toilet is not a toy, and that he can only put things in it when you are with him. You may need to put a safety hook on the lid and put toilet paper out of reach if you think that he is likely to experiment on his own. A few children may seem upset by watching you flush away what they have just produced. If your one-year-old seems bothered by your flushing, skip that step until he leaves the room. An older child can be reassured by explanations of plumbing systems, but a one-year-old can't understand such complexity and is better off with your calm reassurance that you will clean the potty later.

If your toddler doesn't go in the potty, replace his diaper and tell him you'll try again later. Don't make him sit longer, even if you notice that he wets or has a bowel movement five minutes later. He may not have realized that he needs to go, or he may have wanted to wait until he had his diaper back on. If you get mad or insistent, he may resist even more. If you change him calmly and tell him that someday soon he'll be able to use the potty when he wants to, you'll set the stage for him to cooperate when he's ready.

Continue with this stage of training until your child is regularly producing urine or a bowel movement several times a day. It may be days, weeks, or months to reach that point because children are so variable in the way they respond to toilet training. If you are keeping the sitting time to just a few minutes several times a day, you won't be spending more than 20 minutes a day in this activity, but your child will be learning all the same.

Once your toddler has used the potty successfully on many occasions, it's time to take him out of diapers and put him in training pants (padded cloth underwear) during the day, except for naps. However, most children will not be ready to take this step until they are past two years of age. It's not unusual for a one-year-old to get very enthusiastic about using the potty, to insist on being out of diapers, and then to lose interest in the whole process a few weeks later. Parents may be perplexed or even angry, feeling that their child was trained and is now refusing to go. What has happened, in fact, is that the toddler was not motivated enough to continue and is not mature enough to care whether he is wet or dry. In this case, it's best to resume the use of diapers with regular use of the potty and return to training pants again once the child seems ready.

Once your child is in training pants, have him use the potty whenever he wants to, but encourage him to go about every two hours. Praise him mildly for success, but don't scold him when he forgets or makes a mess. Remember that if your one-year-old has gotten this far in toilet training, he is very advanced already, and pushing him to go faster probably will not help.

If at any stage of toilet training your one-year-old becomes very upset, uncooperative, or resistant, either slow down or stop training altogether. If you find yourself getting irritated or angry at your child, that's another reason to take a break. Most children will make a smooth, if slow, transition from diapers to underwear, and the persistent but patient parents will find that their efforts are rewarded eventually!

9

DISCIPLINE

All parents would like their children to behave well, but many parents don't like to use the word discipline. To these parents, discipline means an angry adult pointing a finger at a cowering child. To these parents, discipline simply is punishment.

Actually, discipline means teaching and training, not just punishment. Because parents are a child's first teachers, they will have to discipline their children, one way or another. The important question is: *How* do you want to discipline your child? Children don't automatically act the way their parents or the world would like them to behave, so they must be taught, by you or by someone else. Even though your youngster is only a year old now, you can begin to teach him to be the kind of person with whom you will enjoy spending time and who will be enjoyed by other people as well.

Sometimes parents aren't sure whether they should allow their child to behave in a certain way. Some parents don't want to be too critical or too demanding, perhaps because they feel that their own parents expected too much from them. Other parents may feel that they must be very strict with their child now, or the child will never be able to behave acceptably. If parents don't agree about how lenient or strict they should be, it can be very hard for them to reach an agreement about appropriate discipline.

Here is an approach to discipline and behavior management that can work for you now and that can be adjusted over time as your child grows. Think about balancing your

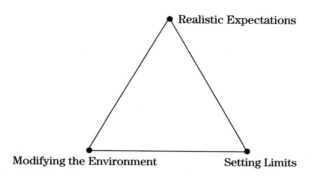

Realistic Expectations

Modifying the Environment   Setting Limits

approach to discipline in the same way that you balance your diet. Milk is a healthy food, but an all milk diet isn't balanced. A healthy, balanced approach to disciplining your child would include three areas, as this diagram shows: realistic expectations, modifying the environment, and setting limits.

Realistic Expectations. To discipline a child appropriately, you need to know what a child his age is like. What can you expect from a one-year-old? You know that you can expect many challenges to your authority! Reading these Keys, especially Part Three—Typical Toddler Behavior and Misbehavior, will help you see whether you are expecting too much or too little from your child. It's also helpful to talk to other parents, to spend time with other one-year-olds, and to observe children of different ages playing together. It's best if both parents learn about toddler behavior together, so that one parent doesn't have the burden of being the expert. When both parents learn about normal behavior, they are better able to support each other's child rearing efforts, to talk over disagreements, and to work out solutions to problems.

Part of being realistic about your one-year-old's behavior is recognizing that although he often may challenge you, he also has a strong desire to imitate you and to seek your approval. When you see your child behaving in a way that

41

pleases you, don't forget to praise him. A toddler won't always do what you want him to, but he'll glow with pride when his accomplishments are rewarded by your smile and words of encouragement. Praise, or positive reinforcement, is a powerful tool for teaching good behavior.

Modifying the Environment. A one-year-old needs an environment in which it's fairly easy to behave well. That means that your house must be childproofed to protect him and your possessions as he explores. You must create places and opportunities indoors and outdoors where he can expend his energy by running and climbing. He is unlikely to be able to behave well if he is expected to sit quietly for long periods or to refrain from touching objects that look interesting to him. A one-year-old also needs some predictability in his day so that he can learn to be cooperative with napping, feeding, going out, and going to bed on time. Last, a one-year-old also needs parents who get an occasional break from him! His intense desire to be independent can make your home feel like a battleground at times, and it's good for parents to get away and have private time to keep tensions at home from escalating.

Distracting your child from misbehaving is a very effective way of modifying the environment. If your one-year-old is causing trouble while you cook dinner, give him a simple task to do or put some water in the sink so that he can splash while you chop vegetables. If he keeps opening all of your drawers to explore the contents, give him a drawer or cupboard of his own with a changing assortment of interesting items so that you can redirect him there. Make games out of activities that he resists, such as taking a bath or getting dressed. These strategies will not always work, but they are a good place to begin and will make your days together more fun for both of you.

Setting Limits. No matter how much you understand your toddler's developmental needs, and no matter how child centered you make his environment, you still will have to set limits on his behavior. That means that you have to have rules in your home. The rules you make should be important enough to you so that you are willing to enforce them consistently, because occasional and halfhearted enforcement usually will lead to more misbehavior from your child rather than less. Parents often find themselves getting angriest at their child in the late afternoon, not because the child suddenly has misbehaved but because the child has been misbehaving all day and the parents finally are worn out! This is called last straw discipline, and it doesn't work very well.

To set limits effectively, parents need to reach a basic agreement on the important rules of the household. Once they have decided what the rules should be, they must be willing to act when the rules are broken. Most parents don't have too much trouble in this area when the issue is safety— they know that a child *always* must travel in a car seat, and *never* be allowed to touch the stove. But other rules may be less clearly defined and enforced, and these are the rules that the toddler will challenge again and again. If you are clear about the rules, you will be able to interrupt his misbehavior quickly and calmly the moment it begins. Rather than giving him warnings or threats, go to your child, repeat the rule, and take action.

For example, if you don't want your child to throw toys and he throws a metal truck at the wall, it's very effective to pick it up, say calmly, "Trucks are not for throwing," and put the truck away. If he throws another toy, do the same thing again. If he has a tantrum, wait quietly (see Key 20). Although you may find it difficult to calmly enforce a rule your child doesn't seem willing to follow, he eventually will get the mes-

43

sage and go on to another activity that is more interesting to him than a calm, boring parent! (Of course, it's also a good idea to keep some soft balls or toys around that he *can* throw!)

There will be times when your one-year-old will misbehave in a way that seems so unacceptable to you that you will want to make a special point of teaching him not to act that way again. Sometimes, just saying "No" in a stern voice will be enough to get a toddler to rethink his activity and change his behavior. However, most parents find that there are times when their toddler is acting particularly defiant or aggressive (see Keys 30–32) and they feel they need to take stronger action.

The best strong action that you can take to stop your child from misbehaving is to use a technique called time out. When you find that other techniques do not work and your child consistently is provoking you, a time out can be an effective and powerful way for you to act.

When your child misbehaves in a way that he knows is breaking a rule, go to him and remind him: "No playing with the lamp cord," or "No pulling the cat's tail." Take your toddler to a place you have chosen to be a time out spot, such as a special chair or the foot of the stairs. Have your child sit in the spot for a very short time—one minute is plenty for a one-year-old—while you stay next to him to keep him there, holding him if necessary. At the end of the minute, let your child return to playing. If he goes back to break the rule again, as many toddlers will, repeat the time out as often as you need to. If you can stay calm and consistent, your one-year-old eventually will realize that his misbehavior is resulting in a repetitive response that interrupts his play, and he will go on to something else.

Using a time out gives you a way of physically taking action when words alone aren't enough. By separating your child from the scene of his misbehavior, he has a chance to change his activity. Because your reaction to his misbehavior is calm and repetitive, he won't find it interesting or exciting to keep provoking you.

A time out is a much better way of teaching your child to behave than slapping or hitting him. Although you may be tempted to spank your child at times, when you teach your child to behave by hurting him, you also are teaching him that he can get his way by hurting others. Children who are spanked regularly may seem to be better behaved at times, but they often grow up to be the kids who only follow the rules when someone stronger is watching.

Try to remember how important your job is as your child's first teacher. A good teacher is creative, using many different approaches to guide a child to learn. A good teacher tries to understand the ways in which each child is different in how he learns, and that children may learn one skill easily and have a hard time with another. A good teacher is patient, even when children are not. Above all, a good teacher, like a good parent, knows that it can take a long time before a child seems to have learned what he has been taught. As a parent, you may not know for sure what your child has learned from you until you see him teaching your grandchildren!

Part Two

TEMPERAMENTAL
STYLE

C hildren are different in many ways. If you spend the morning in a park watching a group of one-year-olds you will see them engaged in many different activities and using many different skills: running, climbing, sitting, examining, listening, talking, laughing, and crying. If you look closer, you will see that the children are acting differently not just in *what* they are doing but in *how* they are doing it. Every child has his own behavioral style that makes him unique.

All parents recognize these differences among children, but many parents think that these differences are only a result of how the children are being cared for by their parents. Many parents do not know that there are also behavioral patterns that can be observed in early infancy and continue throughout life. These patterns are influenced, but not completely changed, by the responses of parents and other caregivers.

Your child's inborn behavioral style will have a big effect on how he learns and interacts with his environment and with you. His style, which also is called his temperamental style or temperament, will determine how easy or difficult he is to care for at different stages of his life. If your child's temperamental style is very much like yours, you may find it easier to understand his behavior. If a child's temperamental style clashes with that of his father or mother, his parents may find his behavior perplexing and unpredictable. No matter what the parents' own style may be, a child with certain temperamental qualities will seem easier or more difficult to get along with at certain stages and in certain circumstances. Whatever your child's temperamental style, understanding it will help you to understand your child much better.

These qualities of temperament were first described and studied by two researchers at New York University, Stella Chess, M.D., and Alexander Thomas, M.D., both professors of psychiatry. By following the development and behavior of 133 babies over the succeeding 30 years of their lives, Chess and Thomas were able to show that a child's inborn temperament was a critical factor in determining a child's overall behavior. Their work has been expanded upon by many researchers and clinicians who work with young children and their families.

There are nine different temperamental qualities that will be described in detail in Keys 10–18. As you learn about these temperamental qualities in the Keys, you will see how recognizing your child's unique characteristics can make it easier for you to understand and help him as he grows.

10

∿∿∿∿∿∿∿∿∿∿∿∿∿∿∿∿∿∿∿∿∿∿∿∿∿∿∿∿∿∿∿∿∿∿∿∿∿∿

ACTIVITY LEVEL

I f you have a very active child, you've probably been aware of his high activity level ever since he was a baby. An active baby doesn't lie still in his cradle. Even in the first early months, an active baby is wiggling and squirming around. Parents put him to sleep in the middle of the crib, and when they check on him later he somehow has maneuvered himself into a corner. When he's awake, he's often lying on his back cycling his arms and legs, or lying on his stomach doing push-ups!

If your child has a very low activity level, you probably noticed long ago his ability to stay in one place. He may have been content to watch the world from an infant seat or to lie on a blanket while activity surged around him. Even when he learned to sit, or crawl, or pull himself up, he probably didn't seem to spend a lot of time exercising his new skills. He probably appeared to be very calm compared to other, more active, babies. You may even have worried if your baby was too quiet as you watched other babies move about vigorously.

Just as some babies are *very* active or *very* quiet, so are some one-year-olds. Because one-year-olds tend to be fairly active overall, you may wonder if it makes any difference what your child was like last year. It does make a difference, because the day-to-day behavior of a child who is naturally very active will be different from the behavior of a child who is naturally quiet. Even though both children may seem to climb and run and move around in the same fashion for *short* periods, the more active child will need to spend more time in energetic play. The quieter child will be able to spend more time in activities that require him to stay seated.

Here are questions to ask yourself about your child to get a sense of how active he is:

- Does my child struggle to get moving while I dress or diaper him?
- Does my child run when he moves through the house?
- Does my child squirm and move around while he is waiting for food?
- Does my child have trouble sitting for long in a shopping cart in the supermarket?
- Does my child fidget when we're having a quiet activity, even though he's interested?
- When my child is playing with toys indoors, does he move about and throw and bang his playthings?
- Does my child enjoy activities that involve moving around more than activities that require sitting?

If your answers to most of these questions are a strong "yes," you have an active child. If you answered "no" most of the time, your child is more quiet. Most parents will have answers that fall in between two extremes but will see their child as generally either active or quiet.

If your one-year-old is active, you will find that daily life is much more manageable if you provide him with many opportunities to move about. Anytime you try to keep an active toddler sitting still, you are in for a struggle. At home he will need space, indoors and out, to run around and climb. If you don't provide him with a climbing structure, he'll use the furniture! It's best to minimize situations, such as long shopping trips or dinners in restaurants, where you will need your child's cooperation to sit quietly. When you take your active child out, be sure to give him time to exercise his muscles before you go in somewhere where he must be quiet. If he can't sit still, it's best to remove him from a situation rather than to try to force him to behave the way you'd like. An active child's movement is not misbehavior. As your child matures, you will be able to help him to vary his activity level in response to the setting, but a one-year-old is too young to have that kind of self-control.

Many active children have at least one parent who is also very active. If your own temperamental style is on the quiet side, you may find your toddler's activity level particularly demanding. If you can remember that the high energy movement of your child can be a real asset as he gets older and needs less supervision, you may find it easier to appreciate him now.

A child who has a low activity level is usually seen as being good because his quiet behavior is easier to manage. Some parents, however, particularly those who are more active, may find that the quiet style of their toddler is at odds with what they expected. A parent may be frustrated in trying to play with a child who prefers to sit in the sandbox rather than running around at the park. It may be annoying to have a child who is able to walk but demands to be carried all the time. Just as the parent of an active child can't force him to sit, you won't be able to get your quiet child to move about. It's much better to adjust your expectations to the activity level of the child you have and enjoy the advantages of this aspect of his temperament.

11

REGULARITY

Regularity is the temperamental quality that describes how predictable your child is in her daily patterns. Regularity applies primarily to physical habits such as sleeping and feeding. Because much of the care of a one-year-old is based on responding to her needs in these areas, it can be very helpful to know your child's inborn patterns.

A child who has a high level of regularity can be expected to go to sleep at about the same time every evening and wake up at the same time every morning. She takes naps regularly and the amount of sleep she requires doesn't vary too much from day to day. She usually is hungry at about the same times every day and may be very predictable in the amount she will eat or drink as well. She has her bowel movements at predictable times, often after meals, and doesn't have any difficulty passing them. She may have developed certain habits, such as having a bottle at bedtime, that seem to be a necessary part of her routine. Although her regularity and predictability can make it easier for parents to plan her day, she may find it difficult to change her routine. She may get very unhappy if her nap is delayed or be unable to wait for lunch if it's later than usual.

The irregular child can be very difficult to plan for day to day. If parents wait for her to act tired they may be playing with her until the wee hours, but that doesn't mean she'll sleep late in the morning. She might take a half hour nap, or she can sleep solidly for an afternoon. It's hard to predict how much or when she'll want to eat. She may eat a big meal, or she may want to have small snacks all day. Her bowel patterns vary and if she goes for more than a day or two without having a bowel movement, her stools may be harder than usual. Although her lack of predictability may be frustrating to her parents at times, they also may enjoy not having to worry about whether she is up too late or misses a nap or a meal, because her schedule changes from day to day anyway. If she is in child care, she may be able to eat and sleep on the same schedule as other children but she may still be unpredictable at home.

Here are questions to answer to determine your child's regularity:

- Does my child seem sleepy at about the same time each evening?
- Does my child wake up at about the same time every morning?
- Does my child want about the same amount of solid food at each meal every day?
- Does my child drink about the same amount of milk or juice at each meal?
- Does my child want a bottle or snack at bedtime every night?
- Does my child have a bowel movement at about the same time every day?
- Does my child usually want to be physically active at the same time every day?

If your answers to most of these questions are a strong "yes," then you have a very regular child. If you answered "no" most of the time, your child is more irregular. Some parents find that their child is more regular in some areas than in others.

If your one-year-old is very regular, you probably have learned to plan your life around her needs. In general, regular children are easier to live with because they are so pre-dictable. However, if your plans conflict with your child's inner clock, you may have difficulty. Regular children can have a hard time when they go on vacation or to special events and their schedules are disrupted. Parents of less regular children may not understand that it is hard for your child to miss her nap or not have a snack in the middle of the morning.

Parents of irregular children sometimes think that their children are just terrible sleepers or terrible eaters until they see that their child's patterns are related to their lack of an inner clock. Once the parents of an irregular child can see that the child is in fact predictable in her unpredictability, they can begin to shape their responses to her behavior in a way that can bring order to the life of the whole family. The irregular child usually responds very well to a gently imposed schedule. By having a regular time to go to bed (even if not to sleep) and to be offered food (even if not to eat), a child learns that daily life is predictable even if her inner rhythms are not. As the irregular child grows up, her lack of an inner clock can even be an advantage, because it allows her to adjust her needs for rest and food according to the demands of her schedule.

One area that can be problematic for parents of an irregular child is toilet training. If your child has very unpredicatable needs and timing for emptying her bladder and bowels, it will be harder for her to adjust to regularly using the potty. If your child is irregular in this area, be cautious about starting toilet training too soon. Although she may have occasional successes, the irregular child may take longer to be consistently dry or accident free.

12

RESPONSE TO NEW SITUATIONS

Children are very different in the way they initially respond to a new situation. Some will respond enthusiastically to new foods, new places, and new activities. Others will pull back and seem reluctant and unwilling to venture into the unfamiliar. For example, one parent may find that if she takes her one-year-old to the house of a friend who also has small children, her child instantly will begin exploring, examining new toys, playing with his new acquaintances, and generally making himself at home. Another parent may find that her one-year-old, in the same new situation, will want to sit in her lap, refusing to look at toys, and perhaps even turning his face towards her to avoid looking at other children. It may take a half hour or even longer before he will venture out to explore. The parent may even find that her child will need to stay by her side the whole time, and will not seem comfortable until he has revisited the new situation several times.

Someone who has not seen enough children to know that they normally have different responses to new situations might not realize that both of these children are behaving normally. Some children have a very positive response to brand new situations. They plunge right in and seem comfortable from the moment they arrive. They can leave the parent's side quickly, even though they may want to keep her in sight as they explore. Other children respond to new situations by pulling away, or withdrawing. They spend a long time holding back, watching but not interacting. They often need to do their watching from the safety of a parent's lap.

Parents and other adults sometimes label the first type of child's behavior as well-adjusted and the second type of behavior as shy. It's understandable that the first type of child would be seen as easier to manage than the second type of child. When the parent of the child who enjoys new situations goes out, he knows that his one-year-old probably will seem to have a good time and will interact easily with others. He knows that other adults will smile and talk to his child and that his child will respond readily. On the other hand, the parent of a child who withdraws from new situations may find it difficult to go out unless he is willing to let his child stay close to him the whole time. The child who withdraws may not respond to other adults trying to engage him, and may pull back even further if they keep trying. Sometimes, other adults who are frustrated by a child's withdrawal will blame the parents: "If you didn't hold on to him so much, he wouldn't have such a hard time." Even though parents may feel that the child truly needs their support, they may wonder if they're doing something wrong.

The reaction of approach or withdrawal from new situations is a natural quality that is a part of every child's temperament. It is a quality that is particularly easy to observe in a one-year-old. That's because a child at this age is so dependent on his parents that the way he copes with leaving his parent's side often is determined by how much he initially is attracted to new experiences.

Here are questions to answer to determine how your child first responds to a new situation:

- Does my child smile right away when an unfamiliar adult talks to him?

- Does my child approach new visitors at home?
- Will my child talk or try to communicate right away with unfamiliar adults?
- Does my child want to explore any new place (a store, friend's house) right away?
- Does my child want to play right away with children he meets outside the home?
- Does my child seem comfortable within ten minutes in most new situations?

If your answers to most of these questions are a strong "yes," then you have a child who has an eager response to a new situation. You probably find it easy to take him out socially and to plan different experiences. Generally, parents who have a child with this characteristic find that there are few problems associated with it. However, it is worth remembering that the eager child is often very friendly with strangers and may wander off to explore an unfamiliar store or shopping mall. He will need to be taught to stay by your side unless you give him permission to walk away.

If your answers to the questions were usually "occasionally" or "never," then your child is the kind of person who often withdraws from a new situation. This characteristic will not interfere with him being successful in social situations, but he will need extra help from you.

The child who withdraws from new experiences has been described as "slow to warm up." This expression is very helpful, because it explains what anyone who gets to know a lot of children can see: The slow-to-warm-up child, if he is given adequate preparation and support for new experiences, can adjust as happily and successfully as any other child. However, it is also true that if a slow-to-warm-up child is pushed or criticized for not being quick to respond, he is likely to become more clingy and withdrawn and perhaps even fearful.

If you feel that your child is slow to warm up, either sometimes or always, take the time to figure out what kind of experiences seem to be the most difficult. Most children will be able to get comfortable more quickly if they are exposed to the same situation repeatedly. If they visit the same friend's house several times, they will take less time to begin playing. Many children will be more likely to join into a small group than a big group, and most will be better able to interact with an adult who doesn't push them to respond. Slow-to-warm-up children are helped when the parent talks to them about where they are going, who will be there, and what will be happening. Even in his own home, the slow-to-warm-up child will need to be prepared for visitors and new experiences. Perhaps most important, the child who withdraws from new experiences needs to have his parents' support and understanding of this temperamental quality. He needs to feel that his parents value him and are not upset or ashamed by his reluctance. If his parents feel good about him, he will feel good about himself, and gradually will build the self-confidence he needs to face the challenge of new experiences.

13

ADAPTABILITY

Just as children are different in the way that they initially respond to new situations, they are different in the way that they adjust to change after their initial response. The temperamental quality that describes a child's rate of adjustment is called adaptability. When an adaptable child tries something new or is put into a new situation, he seems to adjust to the change quickly and happily. The child who is less adaptable, in contrast, will resist different situations even after repeated experiences and takes more time before he seems to accept change. Even though a child is less adaptable than others, he will eventually adjust to change if parents can be patient.

If your child is very adaptable, you will find that once he has tried something once or twice he acts as if he has been doing it forever. For example, if you take him to a new park, he may approach the slide hesitantly on his first visit but the next time you take him there he acts as though he's been playing on it his whole life. If your child is less adaptable, he will need many visits to the park or any new place before he acts comfortable with being there. The key to helping the less adaptable child learn to adjust is to allow him as much time as he needs to feel comfortable.

Adaptability also influences a child's reaction to new rules and routines. A child who is very adaptable will accept rules after a few reminders. A child who is less adaptable will continue to behave as though a rule is new, even though you have told him many times. If you decide to change the bedtime routine of an adaptable child, he may protest at first but he will adjust to the new plan after a few nights. The less adaptable child, on the other hand, will take more time to accept the routine and will protest the change longer.

Here are some questions to ask to get a sense of your child's adaptability:

- Does my child take several days to get used to being in a new place?
- Does my child take a long time to get used to being left with a new baby-sitter?
- Does my child have trouble sleeping in a new place for the first several times?
- Does my child seem uncomfortable with other adults even after he has been with them several times?
- Does my child continue to resist routines like face washing, hair combing, and getting dressed even though we have the same routines every day?
- Does my child continue to misbehave in the same way even though I have set a firm limit several times?
- Does my child continue to challenge safety rules even though he knows that I enforce them consistently?

If you have answered these questions with a strong "no," then your child is probably fairly adaptable. If you have answered with a strong "yes," then it is likely that your child's ability to adapt is very low.

If your child adapts easily to new situations, you will find that this quality makes it easier for you to take him to new places and to change his routines. However, the ease of your child's adjustment to change may allow you to feel as though he can handle more new experiences or disruptions to his routines than the average one-year-old can handle. Even the most adaptable one-year-old will be happier if there is some predictability to his life. A very adaptable child may not let you know right away that he is being stressed by having to adjust to too many changes in his life. Sometimes parents of adaptable children don't realize that they need structure and stability as much as any toddler.

If your child is not very adaptable to new situations, he will do better if you try to keep his days and routines as predictable as possible. Once your child has finally adjusted to a situation, he probably is content. However, because toddlers need new experiences to learn and grow and no family can (or should) keep its routines completely unchanged, you will have to teach your child to become more adaptable. The challenge to parents of less adaptable children is to choose new experiences that give their child opportunities to learn to adjust to change successfully.

You may be tempted to protect your nonadaptable child from all new experiences because he doesn't seem to enjoy them. However, if you continue to expose him to the same new experiences over and over, he is likely to adjust over time. For example, if he doesn't want to try a new food, you don't have to stop offering it. Instead, offer it once a day and wait the weeks or months it takes before he is willing to taste it. If he doesn't want to play on the slide in the park, don't force him, but continue to visit the park and the slide often, so that he can get used to the idea that it might be fun someday.

A common problem for parents of nonadaptable children is that the child resists being left with a baby-sitter. Parents sometimes decide that it's too hard on everyone to leave their child, so the family stays home together all of the time. A more positive approach would be to find a reliable sitter who can care for the child for a few hours several times a week. The less adaptable child will resist being left with the sitter and probably act unhappy for several weeks, but each time he is left he will be getting a chance to adjust to the change. He gradually will learn that even though his parent leaves, his parent returns. His distress gradually will lessen. Although his rate of adjustment may be slow, he still can learn to cope successfully.

When parents of a less adaptable child try to protect their child from too many new experiences, other people may criticize them for being overprotective. It can be very hard to judge the balance between protection and overprotection, and it is likely that most parents occasionally will err on both sides. However, you are the best judge of your child's needs. If he is thriving and happy in familiar situations, it won't hurt him to take his time learning to adjust to the less familiar. By giving him gentle, frequent opportunities to try what is new to him, you will help him learn that even though it is hard for him to adapt, he can learn to do so successfully.

14

INTENSITY OF REACTION

Some children express their feelings passionately. From a very early age, they cry vigorously when they are uncomfortable, and laugh and shriek with delight when they are happy. Other children express their feelings mildly. They whimper softly when they are upset, and coo and smile calmly when they are pleased. These different types of responses are described as the temperamental quality of intensity of reaction.

If you have an intense child, you probably have described her to others as dramatic, or as one parent said, "a little Sarah Bernhardt." You may find her hard to deal with when she is angry or upset, because her cries are so loud that she can't even hear you trying to soothe her. You may find it embarrassing when she has a tantrum in front of family or friends, and you undoubtedly are getting suggestions from them on how you should respond. If you are a fairly intense person yourself, you may have difficulty in keeping calm when your child loses control. If you are milder in the way you express yourself, you may find your child's passion frightening or bewildering. At the same time, you undoubtedly enjoy her intensity when she is happy. The laughter and glee of the intense toddler is irresistibly charming to everyone around her. If you are like most parents of intense children, you may not have realized that her joyful exuberance stems from the same passionate expressiveness as her negative outbursts.

If you are the parents of a generally mild child, you probably don't think of her as having strong likes and dislikes. You may think of her as very easy to manage, because even when she is angry or has a tantrum she expresses herself fairly quietly. If you are similar to her in your mildness, you probably are in tune with the lower key cues she sends to let you know how she is feeling. However, if you or other family members tend to be more intense, you will have to pay special attention to the more subtle way your toddler expresses herself.

Here are some questions to ask and answer about your child to determine if she is intense or mild in her reactions.

- Does my child laugh loud and hard when she is tickled?
- Does my child scream and kick when her temperature is taken?
- Does my child fuss when she is being dressed and having clothing pulled over her head?
- If my child doesn't like a new food, does she make a face and spit it out?
- If my child doesn't get what she wants, does she usually cry or stamp her feet in frustration?
- Does my child get excited by praise and laugh, jump, or yell with pleasure?
- If I interrupt my child's play, does she cry or scream?
- Does my child greet other children or visitors loudly, with much expression of feeling, whether positive or negative?

If your responses to many of the above questions were "yes," "always," or "most of the time," then your child is very intense in her reactions. If your responses to most of the questions were "no," "never," or "rarely," then your child is mild in her reactions.

Keep in mind that most one-year-olds are loud and dramatic, and although their behavior may be unpleasant at times, intense reactions are not that unusual. At times, it is the mild one-year-old who may appear to be different if she doesn't act as angry or upset as other children her age. Whether your child is intense or mild, your most important task as her parent is to learn to respond to the feelings that generate the way she expresses herself, and that isn't always easy.

If your child is very intense, you will not always be able to figure out what she is feeling. She may scream when she is angry or sad because something very upsetting has happened. She may also scream when she is just a little frustrated or annoyed by something that is not a real problem at all. Your challenge will be to respond with comfort when she is truly distressed, but to downplay or ignore her outbursts when she is just being dramatic. You probably will make many mistakes in trying to interpret her reactions, but the more carefully you observe her the more you will be able to judge how to respond.

If your child is very mild, she will be easier to get along with than a very intense child, but she will need your assistance. Because she won't be as loud or demanding as other children, you will need to help her to get her needs met at home and in the world around her. The mild toddler sometimes is ignored, by parents or by other adults. She might be described by a teacher as "No trouble at all," but not get the attention she deserves because more intense children are demanding it all. At this age, you can't teach her to be assertive, so you must be assertive on her behalf. As she gets older, you can teach her to be firm and stand up for herself, even if she does so in her own quiet way.

15

QUALITY OF MOOD

You probably have noticed that some one-year-olds seem to be in a good mood more often than other one-year-olds. There are toddlers who seem to be smiling all of the time, toddlers who often wear a serious expression, and even some toddlers who are scowling much of the time. When adults look at young children, they are likely to interpret these facial expressions as happy, sad, or mad, and they may be right. However, a child's inborn temperament also can determine whether he usually looks happy or sad or mad, and it can be very helpful to parents to figure out what their child's general quality of mood is like before analyzing the meaning of the way he acts.

The temperamental quality of mood, like other qualities, can be observed in the first few months of a baby's life. A baby who has a positive quality of mood usually will be smiling. Even when something distressing happens, he is soothed quickly and begins smiling again. He is almost always cheerful, and when he is not, his parent often assumes correctly that there is a good reason for his frowns or tears. The baby who has a more negative quality of mood, on the other hand, doesn't smile very often, even when he seems content. If he has an extremely negative quality of mood, he may be the kind of baby who seems to fret and complain much of the time, or the kind of baby who is described as "having colic that never went away."

Many babies, of course, are neither extremely positive nor extremely negative in their quality of mood. They seem to smile when they are having a good time, cry or frown when they're upset, and be fairly even in mood much of the time.

Although one-year-olds, because of their developmental stage, are likely to be negative in mood much more often than babies, there are still differences between the child who is developmentally negative and temperamentally negative. Keep in mind that if your child's behavior changes from being generally positive to generally negative, you should look for a reason. The temperamental quality of mood is consistent, and a change in quality of mood can be a sign of illness or stress.

Here are some questions to answer to help you determine whether your child's quality of mood is primarily positive or negative:

- When my child wakes up in the morning, does he usually smile and laugh or is he usually complaining or crying?
- When my child sees a new toy, does he smile or frown as he examines it?
- When my child bumps or hurts himself mildly, does he ignore it or does he cry and fuss?
- When my child is playing by himself, does he smile and laugh or is he more likely to frown and complain?
- When my child is sick, can he be comforted or is he fussy and moody until he is feeling better?
- Does my child seem to be in a good mood almost all of the time, or does he have many days when he seems off or distressed and fussy much of the time?

Your answers to these questions will tell you if your child's quality of mood is generally positive or generally negative, or somewhere in between.

If your toddler has a generally positive quality of mood, you know already how lucky you are. When a child smiles and laughs much of the time, it is much easier to tolerate the inevitable times when the two of you are having a difficult day or are in conflict. Remember, however, that the generally cheerful child, like the highly adaptable child, runs the risk of being labeled as so easygoing that "nothing ever bothers him." Having a positive quality of mood is an advantage for your child in coping with life's ups and downs, but you will have to be especially sensitive to avoid missing the times when he is feeling unhappy but is still acting cheerful.

If your toddler has a generally negative quality of mood, you already have noticed that days together can be difficult. Most parents who have children with this quality say that it can be very stressful to the entire family to cope successfully. If one or both parents generally are positive in their quality of mood, they will find it hard to understand the child who doesn't seem to be cheerful when nothing bad is happening. The parents may feel guilty, frustrated, or even angry. Other parents may recognize the negative quality of mood as similar to their own. If the parent feels responsible or defensive about passing this quality on to the child, it may be very hard for the parent and child to enjoy each other.

Although it will be harder to parent your child if he has a negative quality of mood, you will find it much easier once you can label his behavior as being part of his temperament. If you can accept that your child often may frown or fuss when other children don't, you can avoid blaming him or yourself for his reactions. You can see his serious expression as what is normal for him. One parent described her son, who was a chronic complainer, as "the 'Eyoore' in our family," after the gloomy donkey in *Winnie-the-Pooh*. Her affectionate and humorous label helped her family and others to accept his behavior more easily.

If your child has a negative quality of mood and is also low in adaptability, you will need a great deal of understanding and support to deal with his behavior. Because the toddler years can be challenging anyway, they are particularly difficult for the parents of a one-year-old who is negative in mood as well as in his need to become independent. Try to find a health care provider, teacher, or friend who has experience with children with these qualities and who can help you decide what responses work best.

Keep in mind that the child who doesn't smile very often may not fit the popular image of a happy child, but your child may be happy anyway. You can teach him that he is loved and valued for the person he is. He can learn, over time, that he doesn't have to be laughing and jolly all of the time to let people know that he is lovable. He will learn that he can be a caring, affectionate person and have a good time in life without having to smile all the time!

16

PERSISTENCE AND ATTENTION SPAN

The temperamental quality of persistence describes a child's attention span, the length of time he continues with an activity without needing or wanting to stop. Some one-year-olds have an extremely short attention span, moving from activity to activity in less than a minute, whereas others can stay engrossed in one activity for 20 minutes or longer.

The one-year-old with a short attention span is often very curious about the world around him. He moves about quickly as he finishes playing with one toy and finds another one that captures his interest. If he has difficulty with one task, he will find another he can do more easily and switch his interest in that direction. He is often eager to try new things, although his initial interest may wane quickly. His short attention span may make it easier to control his misbehavior, because you can divert his attention to a new and more acceptable activity.

In contrast, the one-year-old with a long attention span will persist in his play with a single toy or activity for a relatively long time. You probably will enjoy his persistence when he is engaged in an activity that is acceptable to you. However, because toddlers often are interested in pursuing activities that are not acceptable to parents, the persistent child also can be a lot of work. If your child has a long attention span, he will be less likely to give up when he wants to do something that you don't want him to do. He may turn a light switch on and off until you are seeing spots, or refuse to stop emptying a drawer that you have clearly put off-limits. He may persist in doing a task by himself that is so challenging that he winds up exhausted and frustrated by his attempts.

These questions will help you to decide whether your child is persistent and has a long attention span compared to other one-year-olds:

- When my child is playing a game with me, does he stay involved for more than five minutes?
- When my child is playing with a favorite toy, will he continue playing with it for ten minutes?
- If my child is practicing a physical activity such as climbing, jumping, or pushing objects, will he persist for more than five minutes?
- If my child is given a new toy, can he play with it for 30 minutes before losing interest?
- Will my child return to an activity he has been enjoying if he is interrupted by something else?
- When my child sees a new object, will he stop to examine it thoroughly for more than five minutes?
- If my child is learning a new skill such as drawing or stacking or throwing, will he practice for more than ten minutes?

If you found that your answers to many of the above questions were "yes" or "yes, most of the time," then your child is more persistent than the average one-year-old. If your answers were mostly "no" or "no, not often," then your child is less persistent than average. Although persistence, like other temperamental qualities, is a natural characteristic of your child and will be present to one degree or another throughout his life, because the attention span of most one-year-olds is short, it is difficult to determine the strength of this quality until the child is older.

If your child is less persistent than average, you will have to accept that he will not find it easy to stick to an activity at this age. However, you can help him by playing with him in ways that help to increase his attention span. For example, if he is putting blocks in and out of a container and starts to lose interest, you can show him how to pile the blocks in a different way. If you are looking at books together and he gets restless, you can talk about the pictures and make up a story of your own. If you notice that he goes from toy to toy until his room is in a jumble, try setting out just a few toys at a time. If he seems to give up practicing a task easily, give him lots of encouragement for continuing to try. Pay attention to the times when he seems the most persistent, and try to give him opportunities to play in the way that captures his attention the longest.

If your child is more persistent than average, you will enjoy the way he is able to get involved with toys and games for long periods of time. It will be more difficult when he uses his persistence to continue to challenge your limits, make repeated requests, or refuse to take "no" for an answer. The toddler who is willing to spend a half hour trying to fit a piece into a puzzle will spend an equal amount of time asking you for another cup of juice or refusing to put his jacket on when it is time to go outside. As with most temperamental qualities, persistence has advantages and disadvantages for parents who have to adapt to their child's behavior.

17

DISTRACTIBILITY

Some children can be distracted easily from an activity, whereas others can tune out interruptions. Most one-year-olds are fairly distractible compared to older children, but even at an early age you can observe differences among children in this area of temperament.

If a one-year-old is highly distractible, you can interrupt him when he is upset if you make a funny face or sing to him. If he is reaching towards a fragile vase and you quickly show him a toy, you probably can redirect his interest. If he doesn't want you to wash his face, you can make the activity into a game and he will stop his objections. The nondistractible one-year-old, in contrast, will resist your efforts to redirect his interest. If he is playing with a toy and you take it away, he will reject a substitute. If he is involved in an activity, he will ignore you when you try to talk to him or capture his attention. If you try to wash his face and he doesn't want you to, he will complain until you're finished.

Answering these questions will help you to decide if your child is more distractible or nondistractible:

- When my child is playing, does he look up if the doorbell or telephone rings?
- If my child is hungry, will he keep eating even if there is conversation and activity around him?
- If my child is playing with a toy, does he look up every time someone comes in the room?
- Will my child continue to look at a picture book with me even if there are distracting noises, such as car horns or doors slamming?

- If my child is playing in the park, does he look up every time someone passes by?
- If my child is crying, can I distract him by singing or talking to him?
- If my child is playing with a forbidden object, can I substitute an acceptable toy without him objecting?

If your one-year-old does seem to be very nondistractible, you already have noticed that there are both benefits and problems that go along with this characteristic. The nondistractible child usually is very easy to manage when he is engaged in an activity that he enjoys. He can play with just one or two toys at a time and doesn't need to explore every item in a room. If he is also persistent, you will feel as though you can get a lot of your own work done while he is happily occupied. When you want to play a game or read a story to him, he stays engaged and interested, even if there are interruptions. Of course, you probably also have found that when you would like to distract your child, it isn't easy. If he wants to play with another child's red truck, he won't accept the yellow one you offer him. If he is splashing happily in the bath, he will be furious at you for wanting him to get out. It is very hard for the parents of the nondistractible child to get him to stop one activity and go on to another, even if it is something he enjoys.

If your child seems nondistractible, try to enjoy the positive aspects of this trait so that you can put up with the negative side. Make sure that when you want to capture your child's attention you are very firm and clear in your approach. Walk up to him, speak slowly, and look him in the eye. If you don't make eye contact, assume that he hasn't heard you at all. Don't get into the habit of nagging him to do things, or he will learn to tune you out even more. Try to give him advance notice to prepare him for what is happening next. For example, you can say, "You have three more minutes in the bath and then it is time to get out." When the time is up, ask him to get out, but if he doesn't stop playing, drain the tub and take him out. He may run back, but the water will be gone. This type of technique will work over time to help your child pay attention to the limits you are setting. He won't become distractible, but he will learn to pay attention to you when he hears the tone in your voice that says, "I mean business."

If your child seems very distractible, you can help him by keeping the level of stimulation around him at as low a level as possible. When he is engaged in an activity, try not to interrupt him. Don't offer him a toy when he's already playing with one. If he seems to have trouble playing with his toys for more than a minute, you can slow him down by having fewer things out at a time. A highly distractible child can get overwhelmed if he has too many choices. You will find that it is easy to distract him from misbehavior, and it can be tempting to never say "no" but rather to always redirect his interest. However, you'll eventually run out of creative ways to get him interested in something new, so you might as well say "no" when you want to!

Sometimes parents of a very active and very distractible one-year-old worry that their child is hyperactive. If you are worried about your child, do consult your health care provider. Although hyperactivity is virtually impossible to diagnose in a one-year-old, someone who sees a great many children of this age will be able to tell you if your child's behavior is within the normal range. If your child's activity and distractibility is unusually high, you will be able to get some practical suggestions for modifying and controlling his behavior so that you can enjoy your time together more.

18

SENSITIVITY

I f you have a one-year-old who seems to be very fussy and particular about small details, you may have a child who is temperamentally very sensitive. One-year-olds tend to be fussy and particular anyway, but a toddler with a low threshold of sensitivity is even more extreme in her likes and dislikes.

A very sensitive one-year-old is striking in that she notices small differences in ways that surprise you. She might have a favorite food that she loves, but if one day you substitute an ingredient she can taste the change right away. She chooses clothing that is of a certain color or a special fabric. She may even notice how you look and be in tune with your mood even when you aren't aware that you are acting differently. A very sensitive one-year-old can often remember contents of rooms or pictures in a book long after you would have expected her to forget them, because she pays attention to details.

A less sensitive one-year-old doesn't seem to mind what she eats, what she wears, what you say or what you do. She isn't completely insensitive once she notices something is different, but it takes a much bigger difference for her to pay attention. Her threshold of sensitivity is much higher than the toddler who seems to be so particular. Although she may not seem to remember details as well as the more sensitive child, her lack of memory usually is due to her not having noticed details in the first place.

These questions will help you to decide if your child has a threshold of sensitivity that is lower or higher than most other one-year-olds:

- Does my child react if I mix a small amount of a disliked food in with a food she likes?
- Does my child notice if I change the brand of milk or juice or another liquid that I serve her?
- Does my child seem to resist playing outdoors on days that are very hot or very cold?
- When my child's diaper is wet or soiled, does she want to be changed right away?
- If my child spills something on her clothing, does she want to put on something dry?
- Does my child like to wash her hands when they are dirty?
- Does my child notice and react to odors such as perfume, food cooking, or smoke, whether they are pleasant or not?
- Does my child refuse to wear clothing that isn't soft or is a little tight?

If your answers to these questions are a strong "yes," then it is quite likely that you have a child with a low threshold of sensitivity, one who truly notices how things look, taste, smell, and feel. However, because most one-year-olds tend to be particular in these areas, it may be too soon to tell if this characteristic is temperamental or due to her stage of development. On the other hand, if your answers were mostly a strong "no," then your toddler probably will continue to have a higher threshold of sensitivity and be less fussy and particular than other children as she gets older.

If your child seems very sensitive, it is helpful to sort out the kinds of details that are especially important to her. For example, if she is very sensitive to taste and texture of food and consistently chooses her favorites, you may have to offer her a more limited variety of foods. If she chooses soft sweatpants every day and gets very upset by the feel of a stiff ruffle, you may not be able to get her dressed up the way you would like to. If she cries when she smells you slicing onions, you may have to do your slicing when she is out of the room. Although this sensitivity may be troublesome to you at times, it is evidence that she is noticing details and is very aware of her surroundings. This sensitivity will make her a very interesting child and grown-up, even if it is more work for you now.

The toddler with a high threshold of sensitivity usually is very easy to manage. She doesn't care what she eats, what she wears, or how she looks. You may find it very simple to meet many of her daily needs. Every advantage has a disadvantage, of course, and your easygoing toddler may one day be the child who doesn't notice that she needs a bath, or that her hands are sticky, or that her room smells like dirty socks!

Part Three

~~~~~~

TYPICAL TODDLER BEHAVIOR AND MISBEHAVIOR

One of the biggest challenges for the parents of a one-year-old is that much of the typical behavior of a child at this age would be *mis*behavior in an older child. If you aren't sure what behavior to expect, it's hard to know what kinds of reactions you should have as your toddler finds new ways to explore his world and challenge all of your limits. Sometimes parents feel that the behavior they see in their one-year-old has to be changed immediately or the child will act that way forever. Other times, they may ignore a behavior they don't like, assuming that the child will outgrow it on his own. In the Keys that follow, you'll read about many different types of toddler behavior and misbehavior, and suggestions for how parents can respond. You'll see that sometimes it's better to help your child by setting limits, and sometimes it's more helpful to take a relaxed approach. You'll see that you can teach your child to behave better or differently in some ways, but that you may have to wait until he's older to teach him in other ways.

As you read these Keys, you'll learn a lot about the behavior you are seeing in your child right now. You'll also learn about behavior that may be typical for one-year-olds in general but doesn't apply to your child. At times, you may look at other children who seem to behaving better than your own child and wonder why. It's quite likely that, at times, other children's parents are looking at your child and wondering the same thing! It would be unusual for a child to have difficulty in all of the areas described in these Keys, but it also would be unusual for him to have no difficulties at all. In fact, many of the behaviors and misbehaviors you'll read about may appear as your child gets older, perhaps even past his second birthday.

The Keys are organized into three parts: Getting Along with Parents (Keys 19–28), which describes the kinds of behaviors that often are related to your child's conflicts about being dependent on you at a time when he wants to become independent; Getting Along with Others (Keys 29–33), which describes the kinds of behaviors you may see as your toddler is out in the social world; and Habits (Keys 34–38), which describes the kinds of patterns that many children exhibit as they pass through this stage of development.

GETTING ALONG WITH PARENTS

As you read in Part One, one of your one-year-old's important tasks this year is to start to become independent from you. His ability to feel good about himself as a valued and loved person was nurtured by the way you cared for him when he was a baby. If he felt that he was surrounded by loving, trustworthy adults who responded to him when he needed them, then he learned that he was someone who was very important. This feeling of self-importance will be the foundation of healthy emotional growth and development for the rest of his life.

All the love and care you gave your one-year-old last year now gives him the strength to strike out on his own. It may seem absurd to think about a toddler's quest for independence when he is still so needy of his parents. But if you compare his helplessness as a newborn to his abilities today, you can see that he has in fact become more independent of you already.

As your toddler grows, his need for independence will cause him to behave differently towards the people on whom he is most dependent. He will assert himself towards his parents, many times in a negative way. When the pressures of trying to be independent overwhelm him, he will cling to his parents for protection. As a saying goes, "When the comfort of the garden is not enough, there is always the challenge of the world. When the challenge of the world is not enough, there is always the comfort of the garden."

In the following Keys, you will read about the many ways that your toddler may show you his changing needs for comfort and challenges, for dependence and independence. There is no timetable your child will follow in this area of development. Although many toddlers go through these stages before they turn two years old, others may wait until they are closer to three. Just remember that the one-year-old who doesn't act this way is not "good" compared to the one-year-old who does. Normal, healthy toddler behavior includes negativity, rebelliousness, resistance, and assertiveness. Your child will need to go through this stage at some point in his own way to become independent of his parents.

19

NEGATIVITY AND OPPOSITIONAL BEHAVIOR

One day this year your one-year-old will look at you and say, "No!" She may look mad, she may look serious, or she may look playful. You may not know what to say or do when you hear your child use the word that gives her a new kind of power.

Even though your toddler's saying "No" is a symbol of her increasing ability to tell you she has a will of her own, she probably has been saying "No" to you in nonverbal ways for months. Do you remember the first time she pulled back from a spoonful of food you offered her and shook her head from side to side? One psychologist has speculated that this movement of an infant to avoid the parent's spoon is the way we all learn to interpret that shake of the head as meaning "No!"

Once your one-year-old can say "No," you probably will see an increase in the number and variety of ways she resists you. The term *oppositional behavior* has been used to describe this resistance, because at times parents feel that whatever they suggest, the child wants to do the opposite. Parents who try to avoid the resistance may feel as though whatever they do they're wrong. As one parent said, "I asked my one-year-old if she wanted a cookie. She threw herself on the floor saying, 'No! No!' I finally found out she wanted a cupcake like she had a week ago, but we didn't have any. I couldn't figure out how to make her happy."

If you try to please a defiant one-year-old, you probably won't be successful. The more absurd and trivial her demands are, the less likely they are to be ones that you can fulfill. In fact, if you keep attempting to please her, you may find that she simply increases her demands until you are exhausted, angry, and finally willing to say "No" to her as well.

However, you don't need to be so strict with your toddler that you wind up challenging her into a battle of wills about issues that don't matter. That battle has no winner. If you force your child to give in, she will feel angry and resentful. If you decide to give in, you will feel silly for taking on the issue in the first place.

One strategy that often works to avoid head-on collisions is to offer your one-year-old a choice between two realistic options. Instead of asking, "Do you want milk?" ask, "Do you want milk in the red cup or the blue cup?" Instead of, "Do you want to go shopping?" ask, "Do you want to go to the store now or after a story?" Don't ask her to make a choice that isn't reasonable: "Do you want to take your nap now or later?" isn't a fair question to ask an overtired and cranky toddler. Offering choices is one way to avoid some negative responses, but it won't always be practical and will not help you to avoid ever having to deal with your child refusing to cooperate.

If parents can treat their toddler's negativism as a part of normal daily life, they find it easier to stay casual and matter-of-fact when they are faced with an outburst. When your one-year-old says, "No!" check to see if she is resisting something that she is reasonably within her rights to resist. If she refuses to eat her cereal, or to wear her pink socks, or to kiss Aunt Evelyn, you'll want to respect her "No!" But if she refuses to sit in her car seat, or to let you change her diaper, or to put down the scissors she found in the desk drawer, you'll have to be firm. No matter what the issue, it helps to stay calm. Most parents try either to give their child a brief explanation of why she can't have or do what she wants, or ignore her protests and get on with their activities. As you watch your toddler's reactions to these different responses, you'll figure out which ones work best for both of you.

Occasionally parents are told that a toddler learns to say "No!" because she hears it from others, and that if parents can avoid confronting their children with the "N" word they won't hear it directed back at them later. This advice sends parents the message that their toddler's defiant "No!" is something bad to be avoided. In fact, your toddler's saying "No!" is an important sign that she is becoming her own person, willing to take the risk of defying the parents she loves and needs. It may be too much to ask parents to enjoy this stage of development, but it is a stage that should give you the satisfaction that your child is ready to begin becoming independent.

20

~~~~~~

TANTRUMS

We all know what a temper tantrum is. Most of us have seen one, and some of us can remember having one ourselves (maybe not too long ago). A temper tantrum is the expression of anger and frustration by yelling, shrieking, or screaming. Sometimes a temper tantrum also can involve hitting and kicking or other physical behavior. When a one-year-old erupts into a temper tantrum, parents may wonder how they have failed, or why their otherwise happy child is acting so outrageously. Some parents may be so disturbed or frightened by their child's tantrums that they try to avoid them by soothing or placating the child immediately. Other parents may become angry themselves and yell and scream at the out-of-control child.

Most toddlers eventually will have temper tantrums. Some will have had their first tantrum by twelve months, others not until they are past their second birthday. There are several reasons why tantrums are common in this age group. If you understand the causes of tantrums, you'll be able to handle them better.

The first reason for a toddler to have a tantrum is because he wants something that he can't have. Until now, he was a baby whose needs were met by his parents. He doesn't know that his needs are beginning to be more complex and harder to meet, and he doesn't see why his parents might now want to say "No" to him. He still sees himself as the king of his world, and when his servants defy him he's furious. He doesn't understand these angry feelings and he hasn't yet learned to control them, so he has a tantrum.

Another common reason for a toddler to have a tantrum is because he is frustrated at not being able to communicate verbally. Even if your one-year-old can say some words, he understands more ideas than he can express to you. When he wants to tell you something and he doesn't know how, he gets mad at himself and you for his inability to communicate. When your child has a tantrum for this reason, you may be feeling similarly frustrated. As a child learns to say more words, the number of tantrums he has will decrease.

Parents of toddlers often want to know how they can prevent temper tantrums. Some tantrums can be prevented or avoided, but not all of them, because many of the frustrations of the developing one-year-old come from his own internal conflicts. It's reasonable to try to minimize the number of tantrums rather than to try to eliminate them entirely.

If your child is having temper tantrums every day, see if there is a pattern. Some children are more likely to have a tantrum when they are overtired, either because of not getting enough sleep the night before or because they are overdue for a nap or bedtime. Other children get more fragile when they start to get hungry, and parents find that by offering snacks and meals regularly throughout the day the number of tantrums is decreased. Some children will seem to have temper tantrums after they have eaten certain foods, especially processed foods with chemical additives. Although there is no research that shows that these foods cause tantrums in all children, some parents can identify the foods that negatively affect the behavior of their own child, and these foods should be avoided.

Some one-year-olds have temper tantrums when they have to make a transition from one activity to another. Even if the new activity will be something they enjoy, it is hard for them to let go of the activity in which they're already engaged. A common pattern at this age, for example, is for a toddler to have a tantrum when his mother tells him it is time to get into the bath, and then another tantrum when she tells him it is time to get out of the bath! Preparing your child for transitions by giving him a few minutes warning may help, but probably won't eliminate all resistance.

One-year-olds have difficulty making choices, and that difficulty can lead to tantrums. For this reason, the parent who asks her child, "Do you want vanilla ice cream or chocolate ice cream?" may find herself dealing with an unexpectedly furious reaction. The toddler may want to make a choice, but can't.

Some children will send clues that they're about to have a tantrum. A certain look, a change in the tone of their voices, or some other behavioral cue gives the parents a warning that a tantrum is brewing. If you can catch your child before a tantrum begins, you may be able to distract him with humor or a change of scene before it's too late.

Nevertheless, no matter how observant or careful you are, your child will have some temper tantrums. That is because a one-year-old needs to get angry sometimes, and the healthy expression of his anger will involve letting you know how he feels. An older child can say, "I'm angry!" but a toddler cannot. When a tantrum does occur, don't feel that you have failed or that your child is rebelling unfairly—this is another part of life with a one-year-old.

The key to managing your child's tantrum is to stay calm. Your child needs to learn that when he is out of control he can count on the grown-ups around him to take care of him. If you lose control, he will become even more agitated.

If you try to stop him by yelling at him or hitting him, he will learn that yelling and hitting are the right ways to express anger. If your child tries to hit or kick you, back away, but don't take his reaction personally. If he throws an object, remove any other objects from his reach. Let your child cry and rage as long as he needs to, but stay nearby. If he continues for more than a few minutes, you can attempt to comfort him, and some children will welcome your doing so. Other children will push you away until they are ready to wind down on their own.

There is no good way to stop a tantrum once it has begun, but there is one wrong way. Don't give in to your toddler's tantrum. You may wish that you hadn't said "No" in the first place, but if your toddler learns that he can use his rage to make you do what he wants you soon will be dealing with more tantrums, not less.

Once your child calms down, let him know that you understand how mad he was, but continue on as if the tantrum was just a minor interruption. Your toddler doesn't know how he looked, he only knows how he feels, and when the moment of anger is over, he's ready to move on.

You may find that once your toddler begins a tantrum you get very upset or very angry. You may want to stay calm, but you can't. After the tantrum has ended, you feel guilty about the way you handled it and as exhausted as if you had had the tantrum yourself. If you feel this way, the next time your child begins a tantrum try to count slowly to a hundred, take some deep breaths, and leave the room. Call a friend, or your partner, or a parent advice telephone line. You won't be the first parent to feel overwhelmed by the fury of a one-year-old, and talking to someone can help you to calm down. As you stay calm, your child will be able to calm down, and you both will survive this phase of normal development.

21

CLINGING TO PARENTS

As you watch your one-year-old blossom into an independent child, you will see his emotions swing on a pendulum from defiant resistance one moment to anxious clinging the next. Your brave little explorer toddles off fearlessly, but a loud noise frightens him and he clutches your leg as though the world were collapsing under his feet. Walking down the street, he runs away from you, laughing with delight. You call him back, but he won't come, and acts as if he can't come. He needs you to come to him, and stands there crying until you do.

A one-year-old clings to his parents, and then lets go. If you hold on to him too tightly *he* wants to break away, but if *you* let go before he's ready he will cling even more tightly. It can be difficult for parents to interpret what their child is feeling or needing at these moments, because the child himself doesn't know.

It would be easier for parents to help their children to reach independence if the path were straight and the progress was steady. Instead, children take a step forward, sometimes a leap, and then fall back. As they master one area in their lives, they often lose ground in another. Right after your one-year-old learns something new and exciting, he may need to curl into your lap and be a baby again, as if to gather strength from you to get ready for the next challenge.

When toddlers are learning about the world around them they often develop fears. Their fears may not seem logical to parents who know that their child is not in danger. However, it is hard to know what a toddler perceives as a threat, because his experience in the world is so limited. A loud noise hurts his ears, so isn't that bad? A clown looks different than a real person, so what might he do? A toddler will cling to his parents for protection when he is frightened, and parents must let the child know he can count on them. It doesn't help to tell a toddler, "Don't be afraid." He can't control these emotions. Most of the time, if parents stay calm and allow a child to gradually get comfortable with a new experience, a toddler will begin to feel safe. It may be some time before he is brave enough to let go of you, and you may need to avoid some situations that he is too young to handle. As he gets older, he can learn that a loud siren is for letting people know a fire truck is coming, and that clowns are real people with makeup and masks, but a one-year-old is very young for such explanations. He just needs to feel safe.

Some one-year-olds cling more to their mothers. The mother is often the child's primary caretaker, so he turns to her when he is feeling unsure of himself. If she is not available, he may act more independently but then cling to her when she comes back. A mother may be told that she is being overprotective, and that her child would be more adventuresome if she didn't let him cling. In fact, the toddler may be getting all of his needs met by acting independent while she is gone and dependent when she returns.

If parents feel that their one-year-old is overly dependent on one of them, it's helpful to look at how they usually respond to the child's needs for comfort. There is no simple explanation for the different ways a toddler reacts to each parent, although toddlers do cling more to mothers than to

90

fathers. It may be that the toddler uses his relationship with his mother to "refuel" himself for the challenges of the world. It may be that a mother is more willing for her toddler to be babylike than the father is, and so the child actually needs to cling more to one parent because the other won't let him. Sometimes a mother is more comfortable with a toddler's babylike qualities than she is with his need to be loud or active. A child may sense this response and try to act the way that pleases her, saving his other side for the other parent. If parents feel that their relationship with their child is out of balance, a good first step is to adjust the amount of time the child spends with each parent. Even if both parents are working away from home, toddlers often depend more on their mothers for care. To decrease that dependence, fathers need to become more involved in their one-year-old's daily life, and mothers need to be supportive and willing for them to do so. If your toddler seems to have a case of the "mommies," it can help to plan outings when dad and your child can have time on their own. If your toddler learns that dad is fun and can take good care of him without mom's help, he'll gradually let go of his preference for her.

22

SEPARATING FROM PARENTS

I t's hard to say good-bye to someone you love. Whether you are a one-year-old or an adult, separating from the people with whom you are emotionally bonded causes you to feel some sadness, even if you know that you will see them again. As adults, we can fully understand time, distance, and the reality that our loved ones continue to exist even when we can't see them. This knowledge helps us to manage our feelings so that we can get on with our daily lives after saying good-bye. A one-year-old doesn't have the ability to know for sure where her parents are when she can't see them. She is just learning that they don't really disappear, and as she gets closer to two years old she will be able to remember them and what they do together well enough to use her memories in her imaginary play. But her ability to understand that a separation is not the same as a permanent loss is still very fragile.

One of the tasks for you and and your toddler to master is learning to say good-bye to each other. You and your toddler need to learn how to feel sad, cope with your feelings of sadness, and then be reunited. Some parents, understanding that separations can be hard for one-year-olds, choose to postpone leaving their children at all until they are older. For most parents, that is not a realistic choice, but if it is yours, you still will need to deal with teaching your child how to separate. Most young children need time and help to learn to say good-bye, whether they are babies or kindergartners.

You will be helping your toddler to feel comfortable with your leaving her if she has time to get to know the person who will be caring for her while you are gone. As you read in the Keys on temperament, children are different in the ways that they accept new experiences and adjust to change. One eighteen-month-old might be comfortable being left with a baby-sitter after playing with her for an hour. Another toddler the same age might be distressed until she has met and played with the sitter many times. This different type of reaction doesn't mean that one toddler is less attached to her parents or that the other toddler is more fearful about separation. Each child does have differing rates of adjustment, and as parents you will want to respect these differences as you make plans to leave.

Because your toddler's ability to remember you and her usual environment is limited, it makes sense to avoid making too many changes at once when you need to leave her. For example, if a sitter is coming to your home, you can have the sitter arrive at a time when your one-year-old is ready to play. After they have had time together, you can show the sitter your routines, showing your toddler as well what will happen while you are gone. Make sure that your child has her familiar security blanket or stuffed animal to make her feel safe. When it is time for you to leave, gather your things and say good-bye, even if it causes your child to cry. If you try to slip away while she is busy, she will not be able to make the connection that you have left the house, and she may believe that you have truly disappeared. For this reason, always try to leave when your toddler is awake unless the sitter is one she knows very well.

If your one-year-old seems very distressed or you know by experience that she adjusts slowly to change, keep your first absence short. Your toddler learns by repetition. Every time you leave she will be sad, but every time you return she learns that you do come back. If a toddler is very unhappy about being separated from her parents, it is best to try to find a regular sitter who can come in several times a week for a short time. After several weeks, the slow-to-adjust toddler will be more accepting of the caregiver, and you can lengthen the amount of time you are gone and make the schedule more flexible.

If you are leaving your one-year-old in someone else's home or in a child-care program, your separation will be eased if you make the transition slowly. You can begin by staying with her on her first visit, then by staying for part of the time that she is there, and then gradually increase the hours that you leave her. Most children benefit by this gradual adjustment, but not all caregivers support parents in staying with their child. Sometimes parents are told that their child will be better off if they leave quickly and let the staff deal with the child's tears. However, if a one-year-old doesn't feel that her parent is connected to her experience in child care, she may feel even more alone. Try to find caregivers who can help you make a plan that is sensitive to a toddler's need to make a gradual transition.

Don't be surprised if you feel as sad and distressed about leaving your one-year-old as you expect her to feel about letting go of you. The bonds of attachment are strong. However, some parents have reported feeling terrible about being away from their toddler all day but feeling even worse when they found out that their child seemed happy without them! Although this experience is common, the child who seems happy all day should not be seen as one who doesn't need or miss her parents, but rather as one who is successfully coping with separation.

Sometimes a parent will return to find a toddler so involved with another activity that she ignores the parent's arrival, or worse, has a tantrum when the parent tries to interrupt her. These reactions can be very upsetting to parents, but they are a reflection of a child's need to make the transition between caregiver and parent in her own way. A toddler doesn't need to be rebellious against a caregiver to assert her independence. She also won't feel angry toward a caregiver for leaving her, the way she might feel angry toward you. So when a parent arrives, all of the mixed up emotions of the one-year-old can be released, in a variety of ways. If you don't expect your reunions to be always joyful, you'll be able to adjust to your toddler's way of letting you back into her day.

The best way to reunite with your child after a separation is by giving her your full attention. For working parents, that means coming home and ignoring the mail, the phone messages, and the need to make dinner. Parents of young children consistently report that if they play or cuddle together for 15 minutes when they first come home, the children seem to settle in and are able to allow the parents to get settled as well.

If you can think of separations as necessary although sometimes difficult experiences for both parents and children, you will be able to look at the positive aspects of your time away from each other. You don't have to feel that leaving your child is simply to give you time to work or have time for yourself. Your child also will benefit by having the opportunity to form new relationships. A one-year-old's life is enriched by getting to know other loving adults and having the stimulation of new experiences. If you take the time to help your child learn to separate successfully, you will be setting a good foundation for her to feel safe and secure when you say good-bye.

95

23

PLAYING INDEPENDENTLY

Every parent of a toddler wishes that he could play by himself. As you read in the Keys on temperament, children differ from one another in the length of their attention span and their ability to persist in an activity. Some toddlers are drawn toward solitary play more than others. However, there are ways to help your one-year-old expand the time he can play alone.

As you have learned, your one-year-old's biggest internal struggle is between his desire to be dependent on you and to achieve his independence at the same time. For this reason, he finds it very hard to play on his own when your attention is taken elsewhere. You probably have noticed that if you are picking up toys, your one-year-old is happy to play on his own, perhaps dumping some toys out while you put others away. However, if the telephone rings, your busy toddler is likely to interrupt his play and come over to you, screaming to climb into your lap. He wants you to stay by his side so that he can ignore you!

The more that your one-year-old can feel the security of your presence, the more that he will venture out on his own. That doesn't mean that you should play with him constantly. Instead, try to spend time with him in the same room, being companionable, but not giving him your full attention. You can do an easy task, such as peeling vegetables, making lists, folding laundry, or perhaps visiting with a friend who doesn't have a child but enjoys yours. Your toddler will not play separately from you for more than a few minutes, but if you choose a task that he can interrupt easily, he will start to feel more comfortable about playing independently for longer. As your child gets more used to the idea that he can be with you but not interact with you every moment, he gradually will expand his ability to play alone.

Of course, there will be many times when you can neither play with your child nor let go of work you have to do. It's helpful to have a special basket or drawer in every room that contains a few toys or interesting objects to explore. You can talk on the telephone longer if your child knows that when the phone rings he will be allowed to rummage in a desk drawer with paper and crayons. If you keep conversations short, and praise him for playing quietly when you are done, you'll eventually be able to make or receive several calls a day.

If you are working in the kitchen, have an area away from the stove where he can play while you cook. If possible, give him a drawer with his own real utensils and containers to play with. Because toddlers want to imitate their parents, it can be hard to distract your child with toy cookware while you are cooking with the real thing. He will be eager to help you with potentially dangerous items, such as the toaster and the microwave, but he does not have the judgment yet to learn when it is safe to use these. It's much safer to set limits on touching these objects in the first place. Keep him from interfering with you by talking and singing together, listening to music, or giving him some plastic dishes to wash in the sink.

Bathtime is a good opportunity for a toddler to play independently while a parent stays in the room. If you put a small amount of water in his bath with lots of toys, you can sit with him while he splashes happily. Many parents find that this is a perfect time to read the newspaper! Of course, you must never leave your toddler alone in the bathroom, even for a moment. A one-year-old can drown in just a few inches of water.

Keep your expectations low for independent play, but set some goals. If your toddler can play for two minutes alone now, try to expand his activity to three minutes by sitting near him and talking about what he is doing. Don't set up expectations that are unrealistic, or he always will be nagging you and you will feel as though he never leaves you alone at all. Most one-year-olds cannot play on their own for more than ten minutes, but if you work gradually toward this time now, he can continue to expand that time as he gets older. Watch your toddler at play for a few days at home and notice how long and under what circumstances he's able to play on his own for a few minutes.

24

PARENTING AS
A COUPLE

When you were growing up, do you remember feeling that both of your parents were taking care of you? Or did you feel that your mother was the central person in your daily life, and your father seemed to be in the background much of the time? Many parents today feel that they missed out on getting to know their fathers because it was the mother's job to raise the children.

Rethinking the traditional family structure and sorting out who does what is a challenge. Fathers who want to do more have discovered that it's a lot of work to take care of a small child, especially if they've never seen a man in that role before. Mothers who are eager to share the parenting role in theory have discovered that it's hard letting go of the desire to supervise their partner. When two parents share child care, they inevitably will have different ideas about how the job should be done. If they can't work out their differences, it's possible that the advantages of sharing will be overwhelmed by the stress of arguing.

If you are already in the pattern of Mom being in charge of child rearing and Dad being the assistant, you can change if you want to.

One step is for Dad to start taking charge of your child on his own, without Mom's help or interference. Mom needs to decide that her partner is a competent, intelligent person and that she won't give advice unless she is asked for it. Dad needs to decide that unless he has a critical problem that a person of his competence and intelligence can't solve, he won't ask for advice! The more opportunities that Dad has to learn how to provide your child with care in his own way, the easier you both will find it to share responsibility.

The other step is for both parents to talk about how they see their roles as parents fitting together. Many mothers sometimes feel as though they should be the central figure in their child's life, even if the father wants to do more. Many fathers feel as though they are willing to do more than they remember their own fathers doing, but they aren't sure how much more. In some cases, the father feels more comfortable as a parent than the mother does. Sometimes parents are in work situations outside the home where one parent has more flexibility than the other for caring for the child. Sometimes relatives, friends, or employers are not willing to accept your desire to share care and are critical of your choices. All of these problems, and many more, can arise as you try to work out a parenting style that is different from the one you experienced as a child. The only way to resolve these problems is to keep talking about them.

Of course, even when parents want to share in caring for their child, it is not uncommon for the child to have his own ideas. One-year-olds, who are feeling the push to be independent, frequently will assert themselves by demanding to be cared for by one parent rather than the other. Sometimes this preference continues for months. Sometimes the preference is for Mom, and sometimes for Dad. Although the preference sometimes can be explained by the child's temperamental style fitting better with one parent than the other, often a toddler makes his choice for no apparent reason. Of course, the parent who is not preferred is likely to feel hurt and rejected. The parent who *is* preferred may feel overburdened with the child's care. If your child seems to prefer one parent, remember that this is a common pattern and try not to worry or blame yourselves. The less preferred parent should plan occasions to spend time alone with your child, because most toddlers will be more willing to let go of their more preferred parent if they aren't given a choice. This phase is likely to pass more quickly if parents can strike a balance between accommodating a child's preference but setting reasonable limits. For example, you might decide that it is acceptable for your one-year-old to have Mommy say good night last, or to get him dressed in the morning, but it is not acceptable for him to demand that only Mommy can pour him a glass of milk. You will have to decide for yourselves where to draw the line, but make sure that wherever you draw it you stay reasonably consistent in your limits.

Even if both parents are involved in caring for their child, it's likely that the mother in the family still is doing most of the housework. This is almost always the case in families where the mother stays home during the day, but it is also true in the majority of families where the mother is working outside the home. In fact, in most families where both parents are employed full-time, the mother provides almost all of the care of the children and almost all of the care of the household as well. There are many reasons for this inequality, some of them personal to the couple relationship, and some of them part of a larger expectation in our society that women should be able to do it all. If you are feeling that this imbalance is a problem in your family, it makes sense to start working to correct it while your child is young. As your son or daughter observes the way Mom and Dad share their daily lives, they will be building their own images of what parents do, who takes care of children and who takes care of the home, and how men and women can work cooperatively together.

25

∧∧

SHOULD A TODDLER SLEEP WITH PARENTS?

Many babies, especially when they are breastfed, wind up spending some of the night sleeping in their parents' bed. Sometimes the baby is brought to bed during the night when she awakens and needs comfort, and stays sleeping with parents until morning. In other families the baby sleeps with the parents throughout the night. If the parents don't mind a baby snuggling with them and the baby seems to sleep well, there isn't a problem.

However, as a baby gets older, one or both parents may begin to wonder, "Are we ever going to sleep by ourselves again?" At this point, parents may start talking to friends and collecting opinions from pediatricians, psychologists, anthropologists, and impassioned advocates of different styles of parenting. The more that the parents hear, the more likely they are to be confused. That is because there is truly no right or wrong answer to the question "Should our child sleep in our bed?" As with many other questions you will ask yourselves over your lives as parents, the answer will be determined by your own needs as adults, your child's temperament, and your own sense of what's right for your family.

If you already are sharing your bed for all or part of the night with your one-year-old you may want to think about some of the issues that can cause problems in the year to come. These issues may not be of concern to you now, or ever, but they come from the experiences of other parents who have slept with their own children over time.

An important concern for many parents is their own need for a good night's sleep. Some parents sleep so deeply that they never notice who is in bed with them. Others find that when their toddler wiggles, they wake up. As you have read the other Keys, you have seen that the demands of an energetic and active toddler are going to require you to be alert and active yourselves during the day. Your one-year-old can take an extra long nap in the afternoon, but you probably can't.

Although most parents begin sleeping with a child in order to help her sleep better, they sometimes find that the child begins waking in the night demanding to be fed or entertained. Parents sometimes are embarrassed to admit that they are taking their child into the living room at midnight to watch old movies, but it happens! If your child is not sleeping well, it's time to rethink your sleeping arrangements.

Sometimes a child and her parents sleep comfortably together throughout the night but the parents begin to feel that they no longer have time for privacy and intimacy with one another. It certainly is inhibiting to a couple's sexual life to have a child in their bed, but the child's presence also can interfere with the couple having time to talk, cuddle, or just be alone together. Often, the toddler falls asleep by having a parent lie next to her. If the parent falls asleep, too, the parent's partner may begin to feel as though the child is taking his place. Parents sometimes have difficulty talking about this issue. It's hard to tell your partner that you feel left out and hurt, especially when your rival is a toddler that you love too. Sometimes fathers will feel so excluded that they move into a separate room, leaving Mom and the child alone.

If you are a single parent, you will have to think about the issue of sleeping with your child in a different way than the parent who has a partner. It's very easy to get so comfortable sleeping with your baby that you may be reluctant to change the arrangement as your child gets older. When a parent and child are living alone together, they often have an especially close relationship, one that is warm and satisfying for both. But as your child starts to feel the need to be herself and to separate from you, she may be feeling torn by her desire to stay by your side all night and her need to become independent. She even may sense that you need her at night more than she needs you, and that can be an uncomfortable feeling for a young child. There also may come a time when you would like to spend a night away from her, or to have company when she wants you to be in bed.

As you make the decision about how your family is going to sleep at night, remember that almost all toddlers occasionally sleep in their parents' bed. You may not want to *always* sleep together, but that doesn't mean that you must *never* sleep together either. What's important is to find the arrangement that is comfortable for all of you.

26

DRESSING AND
DIAPERING

From the time your one-year-old can stand and take a few steps, she's likely to resist being placed on her back to have her clothing changed. Some children will wiggle and giggle and tease, but still let you get the job done. Others will fight to stay upright, kicking and hitting as if you were trying to tie them down and leave them! Because you have to change your toddler's diapers and clothing many times every day, any kind of resistance will be frustrating for you. As with many aspects of your one-year-old's behavior, understanding her motivation while at the same time working around her rebelliousness will get you through this stage most easily.

Your one-year-old feels as though she's in control of her own body when she's upright. When you want her to lie down and be passive while you change her, she resists giving up control. If she's tired or in a more cuddly mood, she may be cooperative. But if she's feeling independent, she fights you. If her reaction provokes you to get mad, she may even find that so entertaining that she tries to provoke you more! Sometimes a parent will get so mad that she will yell sharply or even slap a child resisting being changed. Some children will become cooperative when a parent reacts this way, but others will just resist more. Whether or not a harsh response works, if your toddler can provoke you to lose your temper every time you change her, it's not going to be good for your overall relationship.

The younger one-year-old often can be distracted by a special toy that only comes out at changing time. A music box or a gadget that she can manipulate with both hands may work well. Try putting a small piece of masking tape on her fingers. By the time she's finished pulling it off, you'll be done. Changing her in front of a mirror is another strategy. Let her watch herself and you while you make faces and sing songs.

If your toddler doesn't like lying down, try to change her while she is standing up. It's possible to change all but the messiest diaper in this position. If you do have to change her while she is on her back and she's struggling, put your weight on her upper body and turn toward her legs, using one arm and elbow to keep her still. Have an "I mean business" look on your face, and work quickly!

As your one-year-old grows, she'll become interested in imitating you and learning to dress herself. One strategy for getting her to cooperate is to have her help. Let her gather her clothing and hand each piece to you. Have a special routine or rhyme you say while you dress her: "Over the head, over the nose, pull it down, here it goes!" or any silly songs you sing can make it easier for her to be still. As you get new clothing, choose items that pull on easily and with a minimum of fasteners. Selecting clothes for ease and convenience rather than fashion will make dressing easier.

If you can see this resistance by your one-year-old as part of her overall struggle for independence, not her attempt to ruin your day, you'll be able to get her changed efficiently most of the time.

27

FUSSY EATING AND FOOD JAGS

The typical one-year-old is fussy about what he eats. He may have foods he loves to eat one day and refuses to taste the next. He may become enamored of one food and want to eat it for every meal. As we saw in the chapter on feeding (Key 6), his behavior has a great deal to do with his emerging desire to be independent and to separate from you by saying, "You're not in charge, I am!" His eating patterns often are determined by how rebellious he is feeling, and the more his parent tries to control what and how much he eats, the more he'll rebel. The rebelliousness usually is most strongly expressed towards the parent who feeds the child most often. It's not unusual for a one-year-old to clamp his mouth shut when his mother offers him food, and open up like a little bird for the baby-sitter. It's not that the sitter is more skilled, it's that the toddler doesn't need to show *her* who's the boss!

There are other reasons beyond simple rebelliousness for a one-year-old to refuse to eat certain foods. Most toddlers do not enjoy trying new foods, although if they see a food on *your* plate they may be willing to dare a taste. Don't assume that your toddler won't eat a food. If the same food is presented to him many times, without pressure, he may refuse for weeks and then one day take a bite.

Your child will find that certain tastes and textures appeal to him more than others. It's not unusual for a child to refuse all but a certain brand or flavor of a food, such as yogurt, or to prefer strained orange juice to orange juice with pulp. As your child's tastes become more refined, he will have an idea of how he wants food to be presented, and variations in what he is used to may be upsetting to him. For example, many one-year-olds won't eat lumpy food, and many of them will refuse a favorite food if it is too hot or too cold when it is first presented.

Food jags are a variation of fussy eating that are common in young children. A child discovers a food that he loves, and demands to have it served to him at every meal. You may find that if you can offer him a snack or meal of other foods before he gets very hungry, he'll be less demanding. But if the food he craves is basically nutritious, there is no harm in continuing to serve it. Even though you may think that your child will go off to kindergarten eating nothing but applesauce, these food jags don't usually last more than a few months. One exception to this is the child who doesn't want to eat but is drinking more than 24 ounces of milk or juice a day. If your child fills up on these liquids, he won't have room for other foods and he will seem to be a fussy eater when in fact he's just not hungry.

If the food that your child prefers is a treat food, such as cookies or candy, you can't allow him to choose to eat it instead of other foods. A one-year-old doesn't really need sweets at all, so it might be easier not to offer them. If treats and sweets are always around in your home, you'll have to set a firm limit and stick to it. If you only allow him a small portion, he'll still have room for nutritious foods. In fact, some nutritionists don't recommend withholding dessert to the end of the meal because it teaches a young child that dessert foods are more special than other foods and so are more desirable!

Even though this fussiness is predictable and normal for a child this age, you don't have to try to overcome it by trying to anticipate what your child will like or not like at every meal. If you always are adjusting your child's plate to meet his demands, you will teach him that you think it is OK to be a fussy eater and that you think it is your job to try to please him!

The best approach to take is to provide your child with nutritious foods that you know he likes, even if he prefers the same foods over and over. Most children like bread, rice, cereal, and pasta, so serving these grains usually will guarantee that your child will eat something. Present new foods that are suitable for a one-year-old to handle and allow him to taste and try them at his own pace. Serve him meals and snacks at regular times so that he doesn't have to wait until he's hungry and cranky to be fed. Expect your child to have a bigger appetite at certain times of the day, usually at breakfast or lunch times.

Once you have offered him food, you don't have to do anything more than sit with your child and make mealtime pleasant for him. You don't need to coax him to take more bites or to try to eat more than he seems to want. If he refuses all of the food you offer him, leave him alone. If he is truly hungry, he'll eat when you offer the food the next time.

28

WAKING TOO EARLY

Most children wake up early in the morning and insist that their parents start their day just as early. If your child is one of these larks, you may be wishing you could get her to sleep a little later. By observing her sleep pattern over 24 hours, you can see if some adjustments can change her habits.

The most common cause of rising too early is a too early bedtime. Because most one-year-olds will sleep from the time they are put to bed at night until about 10 or 11 hours later, if your toddler is asleep by 7 P.M. and waking at 5 A.M., she's sleeping about as late as you can expect. If you want her to sleep later in the morning, you will have to keep her up later in the evening. Don't try to make the change in one night. Make the change gradually, ten minutes later each evening, until bedtime and waking up time are at the best times for your family's needs. Don't forget to shift her nap times and mealtimes to match the new schedule. After a few weeks, she will have a new 24-hour pattern.

If your early rising toddler is staying up late already, she may not need as much sleep as the average one-year-old. If she seems cheerful and alert after only eight hours of sleep, she may be ready to wake up. However, it is worth looking at her daytime nap pattern before you resign yourself to getting up early every day. A toddler who is getting enough sleep at night usually will nap for an hour or so in the morning and about two hours in the afternoon. If your early rising toddler is taking a two- to three-hour nap every morning, it's likely that she is in fact not getting as much sleep as she needs at night.

If this seems to be the case with your toddler, you can modify her schedule. When she wakes up at 5 A.M., wait 15 minutes before going in to her. She may go back to sleep. If she doesn't, you'll have to get up with her, but later that morning, delay her nap by 15 minutes. Each morning, delay your responses to her morning wakings by fifteen minutes more, and keep her up fifteen minutes later before her nap. Most toddlers will start sleeping later after a week of this delayed response technique, and their morning nap gradually will become shorter.

If your one-year-old continues to be an early riser despite your attempts to reschedule her, you will have no choice but to adapt and learn to get along with less sleep or go to bed early yourself. It may feel uncivilized to go to bed as early as your child does, but it's a lot better than trying to keep up with her the next day if you're too tired!

GETTING ALONG WITH OTHERS

Most one-year-old children will enjoy going out with parents and having the opportunity to be with people and things that are different from their home environment. When you take your child to a park or to someone else's home, you give him the chance to have fun, to take part in some new experiences, and to learn about socializing. Just as important, as a parent you will have opportunities to talk to other adults, to see how other children act, and to watch how different parents manage their children's behavior. You can learn more by spending time with other children and parents than by staying home and reading any book on child development!

Sometimes parents of one-year-olds aren't sure what to expect of their child when they are in a social situation, and sometimes their expectations may be unrealistic. If you haven't watched a lot of young toddlers at play, you might wonder if the way your child acts now is the way he always will act. Many parents worry that the typical social behavior of a toddler will continue for the child's lifetime, and that the self-centeredness they see now is a threat to the child's later ability to get along with others. If you can remember that this self-centeredness is normal for his age, his behavior will be easier for you to accept and manage.

If you have mostly good experiences taking your child out or having others come to visit, you probably will want to make socializing part of your daily pattern. But if you find that your experiences are not pleasant, you may be tempted to stay home with your child until he's older. Keep in mind, however, that most children learn appropriate social behavior from experience and from being taught by parents, over and over. You may want to choose your outings carefully, but some experience away from home is almost always better than none. Your child may need to have many short excursions to the park or to the house next door before he is willing to leave your lap or go near another child. He may need many reminders that he can play with his own truck but he can't grab someone else's. He may not have the social graces you would like, but you still can have fun.

In the Keys on temperament, you read how different temperamental styles will affect your child's reaction to social situations. However, regardless of their innate temperament, all children will benefit from some positive social experiences. If a clingy child gets to watch other children play, he is more likely to venture forth some day to join in. If a child who grabs toys is reminded not to grab but is redirected to another activity, he is more likely some day to respect other children's possessions. If you assume that your child will have many learning experiences, both positive and negative, you won't be so hard on your child or yourself.

In Keys (29–33), you will read about some of the common behaviors of one-year-olds interacting together. You will learn about the kinds of problems you can anticipate with groups of young children, and ways to prevent some of those problems. You also will read about guidelines for choosing child care for a one-year-old, and about the kind of behavior you can expect from your toddler when he is away from his parents during the day. There is a wide variability in the behavior of one-year-olds, and once your child is spending time with other children his age, you will appreciate how unique he is!

29

~~~~~~

SHARING WITH OTHER CHILDREN

When your one-year-old is with other toddlers, you will see her behave in ways you haven't observed at home. One-year-olds enjoy being with other children, but their play is not the sociable interaction that parents can expect from three- and four-year-olds. If you understand what you can reasonably expect to see in a group of toddlers, you will be able to enjoy yourself more and help your child to gradually learn how to play and share with others.

Think about how your toddler plays when she is at home with you. She probably spends a great deal of time engaged in activities that demand your attention. She wants you to respond to her immediately and she probably is happiest when she tells you what to do, rather than the other way around. She is busy exploring her environment and the objects in it in her own way and at her own pace. Her highest compliment to you, or to a visitor, is to offer a toy. Although she may decide that it is a lovely game to continue to bring you toy after toy, she also may decide that it is time to take away the toys. Of course, an adult doesn't mind having a toy truck deposited in her lap and then removed. However, when your one-year-old wants to play this game with another child who also wants to control the giving and taking, the two toddlers may wind up in a tugging match.

It helps to remind yourself that the give and take that adults recognize as fundamental to social relationships is not something a toddler can understand. If parents begin pressuring their one-year-olds to "share nicely," most toddlers will cling to their possessions, even if the object of their desire belongs to someone else. In fact, some children who constantly are pressured to share will get so anxious about being forced to let go that they will hold on even tighter, becoming more possessive than they would have been if left alone.

Another typical toddler pattern of behavior comes from the one-year-old's desire to imitate what someone else is doing. A toy may be ignored by two children for a half hour, but as soon as one toddler picks it up and begins to play with it, the other toddler wants it for herself. Within moments, quiet play can dissolve into an intense battle. Most of the time, the struggle will be brief, because one-year-olds, despite the passions of the moment, don't attach the larger meaning to these quarrels that their parents do.

That doesn't mean that adults should ignore warring toddlers. Adults need to intervene when children are struggling and to redirect their play, but they shouldn't pass judgment on the behavior as being selfish or aggressive. They simply must tailor their responses to the needs of each child to help them learn to play with less conflict.

If your child always seems to grab from others, she may need to have you stay close by her. If she starts to move in on another child, distract her with a different toy or try to engage both children in playing with you. Helping your child to avoid getting into repeated conflicts gives her a chance to find ways of having fun without being labeled as a bully.

You may have a one-year-old who doesn't seem to mind if another child pushes her aside or takes her toys. She may cry for a moment or simply find something else to do. You may worry that your child is being too passive and feel that she should stand up for herself. In another year, your child will have the maturity and the verbal skills to be able to assert herself more, but at this age it's best to allow her to react in the way that she chooses. If she comes to you for comfort, you can help her to find another activity. If she is very upset, you can verbalize her feelings by saying, "It makes you sad when Jimmy takes your toy." But if you give her too much attention and sympathy, she may figure out that it is more interesting to be the victim than it is to solve problems on her own.

One eighteen-month-old boy in a play group seemed to be so in awe of an older and bigger toddler that he allowed the other child to grab all of his toys without protest. His mother saw the disappointment on her son's face but refrained from getting involved. One day, when the children were playing outside, she saw her son quickly set aside the shovel and pail he was using when he noticed the other child approaching. Her son picked up a plastic car, and the bigger boy, as usual, took it from him right away. Her son went back to the shovel and pail he had been playing with in the first place, and his mother realized that he had figured out a way to solve the problem on his own!

There are ways to teach toddlers about sharing and playing sociably. Long before your child is talking, she is learning from listening to you. You can teach about sharing by using the word when you see her give something to you or someone else: "Thank you for sharing your blocks with me, Jennifer. Do you want them back?" When you play together, take one toy and say, "Will you share this with me?" and if she says, "Yes," thank her. If she refuses, say, "Maybe you'll want to share later." When your toddler wants to taste your food, or wants you to taste hers, label that sharing. Let your child learn that sharing is a nice word to hear, not a word that she only hears when there is a conflict.

To further prevent conflicts over sharing, you can plan ahead when your toddler will be playing with others. As the number of children playing together increases, so does the level of stimulation and potential for conflict. Parents need to stay close to toddlers at play rather than sitting apart and waiting for problems to occur before moving in. If certain toys are very popular, it's a good idea to have several of them. If a child has a special toy she never shares, it's best not to bring it to the group. Having activities that everyone can be a part of, such as water play or messing with play dough, will help toddlers to play together with less conflict. When you take your child on a visit, if she brings a few of her toys from home, the host child may find it easier to share his own. When you leave, be prepared to distract your child from her host's toys by offering a favorite object from home that you've saved for this moment. Don't stop on the way home to buy the toy that your child couldn't let go of—she may be much less interested in it if no one else is playing with it!

Think about this year as the time to teach your child what it means to be sociable, and how much fun it can be to be with other children. Prevent conflict when possible, don't force the issue of sharing, and wait until your child is two years old before expecting her to begin understanding another child's point of view.

30

IMITATING OTHER CHILDREN'S MISBEHAVIOR

You are certain to be delighted when your one-year-old begins to imitate the positive behavior of other children. Many toddlers are inspired to climb up a slide, try doing a puzzle, or begin saying "thank you" after another child shows them how.

You probably will be much less pleased when your toddler imitates the undesirable behavior of her peers. The first time your sweet child spits or throws food or shoves a playmate, you may ask, "Where did she learn that?" If you know that she's seen another toddler do the same thing, you will be tempted to blame the other child for teaching your own child to misbehave.

Although it's true that your one-year-old's choice of misbehavior will be influenced by the other children she observes, you can't protect her from learning to act in ways you don't like. There are just too many normal toddlers misbehaving all of the time for you to be able to shelter your child. If you go to a party and the other children throw cake, so will yours, if not at the party then at home a few days later. At that point, you can respond just as if she had invented the behavior on her own. Set an appropriate limit, but don't worry about bad influences.

You may find that there are some families that you enjoy as friends but with whom you disagree about acceptable toddler behavior. If you find that every time you are with this family your child is getting confused about what the rules and limits are, you may be setting yourselves up for a lot of testing and misbehavior. Older children can learn that different families have different rules, but toddlers can't cope with their parents telling them to do one thing at home and another when they go visiting. If you can't work out a balance between yourselves and the other parents, and your child is having trouble behaving, you may have to stop visiting together for a while.

However, don't fault the other family for teaching your child to misbehave—she would have learned how anyway. In fact, it is quite likely that before you have your own toddler fully tamed, she will have demonstrated her misbehavior to enough other children for their parents to begin blaming you!

31

HITTING AND SHOVING

One-year-old children hit and shove. They don't know yet that these are not nice ways to act toward others. In fact, they often may not be aware that there is another person involved in the hitting and shoving, because they have trouble thinking about other people having feelings like they do. A one-year-old's hitting and shoving is not caused by aggressiveness, anger, meanness, or his desire to be a bully. Hitting and shoving in a one-year-old usually is motivated by his normal self-centeredness or his desire to experiment and test limits. Over time, you can teach him that this behavior bothers or hurts others, and he can learn to control his impulses to use hitting and shoving to get his way.

The normally self-centered toddler sees the world from his point of view, and that point of view only. When he sees an interesting toy, he wants it and goes after it. If another toddler is between him and his destination, he is as likely to plow right over her as he is to circle politely around. What is on his mind is taking a direct, fast route to the toy. He is not capable of considering the effect of his behavior on others.

A one-year-old has limited communication skills. If he notices that another child has a toy he wants, or is standing in his way, he takes the action that makes the most sense to him. He can't say, "May I play with that?" or "Will you move, please?" but he can hit or shove and the other child often will yield.

120

In this way, the hitting or shoving behavior becomes a very useful way for him to get what he wants. There is also another benefit that he learns as he tries hitting and shoving in different situations. The results of his behavior, he discovers, often are very interesting. Sometimes the other child cooperates, sometimes she cries, sometimes a parent yells, and often he gets a great deal of attention for his actions! For the one-year-old who is trying to figure out how the world works and what causes things to happen, this variety of responses is so stimulating that he is likely to continue to hit and shove just to see what happens.

Occasionally a one-year-old will hit and shove other children because he has learned to hit and shove at home. Perhaps he has an older sibling who pushes him around and hits him when he wants something. He may have parents who aren't bothered by his hitting or shoving them, and don't say anything when he acts that way toward an adult. He may be watching television shows with characters who hit and shove. He may have a parent who hits or slaps him and so he thinks that hitting is normal behavior for everyone. It's helpful to look at your toddler's role models for behavior before you try to make changes in his behavior alone.

In order to stop your one-year-old from hitting or shoving others, take some time to figure out when this behavior is most likely to occur. If you notice that he hits others when he is tired, hungry, or overstimulated, then you will want to minimize these times or stay very close to him when you know he's feeling edgy.

Some toddlers are more physical than others in the way they express themselves. They may be big in size and unaware of how much larger and stronger they are than other children. When they move about a room you may think of a "bull in a china shop." They may play well in a park, but hit and shove other children if they are playing in a living room. If your child is like this, it's particularly important not to blame or scold him for bumping into other people or things, because he may not know how much space his body takes up. Instead, try to avoid places where he is squeezed in tightly, or where there are several children and not enough room for him to move about freely.

Watch the reaction of other children to your one-year-old's hitting or shoving them. If they are not upset, then you probably shouldn't be either. Other children can accept this behavior as communication, and they aren't bothered about it the way adults often are. However, you may find that the hitting or shoving tends to escalate if you don't interfere, so that you will want to act even if the victim doesn't mind at first. Some ways to respond are to go sit between the children when the behavior starts, to distract the children with a new activity, or to separate the children briefly, saying, "We don't hit." If you overreact excitedly, you are likely to fuel your toddler's desire to repeat the behavior so he can see you get upset again!

If the other child does react to being hit or shoved, watch your child's face to get clues to how to manage his behavior. He may look surprised or bewildered, or may not pay any attention at all to the child he has hurt. In this case, you need to help him learn that his hitting made the other child sad or mad. Have him look at the other child, and say, "She's sad because you hit her. We don't hit. Hitting hurts." If the hitting or shoving is occurring often, you can use stuffed animals to show him how hitting makes others feel. Have two teddy bears play next to each other having fun, and then make one bear hit the other. The bear who is hurt can cry, and the bear who has hit can say, "I'm sorry." You also can play out the big bear coming in and telling the little bears not to hit or shove. If you take a minute to play this way once or twice a day, your child will make the connections. You don't have to tell him that he is just like the little bear. He learns best by imitation, not by your verbal explanations.

If your one-year-old does seem to understand that his hitting or shoving bothers others but he still does it, he may be testing you to see what the limits are. If you try to ignore or simply distract a toddler who is asking for limits, he will continue to misbehave and in most cases will increase his misbehavior until someone stops him. If this is the pattern you are seeing with your toddler's hitting, you should intervene quickly and firmly every time he hits. It is best to move him away from the area and hold him for a brief time out (see Key 9) while you quietly tell him: "No hitting." By keeping your response low-key but firm and consistent, he will learn that the outcome of hitting isn't exciting or interesting, it's just a boring time out. Even more important, he will know that you have set a limit on his behavior and that he can count on you to control his impulses even when he can't control them himself.

32

~~~~~~

BITING

When a one-year-old bites another person, everyone around him gets upset. There are several good reasons for this reaction. A bite hurts, and even a small toddler can exert enough pressure with his teeth to bruise or break through the victim's skin. Biting often occurs without obvious warning, so the victim and the observers around are taken by surprise. Biting also is seen by many as more intentionally hurtful than the more common hitting and shoving that is part of normal toddler play.

Although parents and other children may be more upset by biting than by other toddler behavior, biting is best managed by understanding its causes rather than simply reacting to the result. When a one-year-old bites, he usually is not motivated by aggressive feelings. Because two- and three-year-old children sometimes bite as a way of expressing anger, most of the advice that you will hear about managing biting is based on the assumption that the child who bites needs to learn not to hurt others when he is angry. In the majority of cases, the motivations of a one-year-old to bite are very different and so your response must be different also.

A one-year-old is still at the stage of needing and wanting to use his mouth to explore the world around him. Toys, fingers, bottles, and every other object he touches are likely to wind up in his mouth. Often, a one-year-old bites another child or his parent because he wants to know what it feels like. Parents sometimes are shocked when their one-year-old starts out by kissing them and then suddenly bites. It is this desire to experiment that causes this abrupt shift. If a toddler's oral instincts are not very strong, he may only bite a few times, especially if the parent reacts by quickly putting the child down and saying, "No biting" firmly and sternly. But the child with a stronger oral focus may continue to bite, not out of aggressiveness but in response to his overwhelming inner instincts. It may take dozens of firm and consistent responses from the parent before he realizes that he is doing something wrong.

One-year-olds also bite when they are bored. Toddlers aren't very good at planning their own activities, and if a one-year-old has finished playing with a toy and doesn't know what to do next, he may bite another child just to stimulate some action. Biting behavior forces adults to pay attention to children, and so it is not uncommon for biting to occur in a play group or child care situation where the adults are not interacting enough with the children. Biting behavior may be the most objectionable way that the toddlers seek attention, but other toddlers in the group also may be misbehaving as well.

Some one-year-olds don't like to be crowded by other children. If they are playing and another toddler gets too close to them, they may bite as a way of telling the other child to back off. This strategy usually works for the moment, so the child does it again, not realizing that he hasn't chosen a positive way of assuring his personal space.

A one-year-old may bite if he is feeling overpowered by other children. If he is spending time in a situation where other children are bigger, more skilled, and perhaps are excluding him, he may bite as a way of showing his own power. The bite is not necessarily an expression of anger, but rather a way for a very young child to say, "I count for something here, too."

The toddler who is inclined to bite may bite even more often when he is feeling tense, tired, hungry, or experiencing stress from a change in his daily routine. The birth of a sibling, a substitute teacher, a new child in his play group, or the pain from an ear infection or teething can cause a child to start biting others.

To control the biting behavior of your one-year-old, your first step must be to observe when, where, and to whom the biting occurs. You can almost always find a pattern to biting behavior if you look carefully. Once you see a pattern, you can focus on preventing biting rather than reacting to it.

It is very helpful to offer your one-year-old something safe to bite. A very oral child should have teething toys that can be handed to him at any time: "If you need to bite, bite this." Your one-year-old may even need to keep a teether in his pocket and be reminded to use it when you see warning signals. If a child who sometimes bites is kissing you, say calmly, "No teeth" to remind him. One nursery school teacher followed a toddler with a biting tendency around for three days, handing him a rubber doll every time she sensed he was going to bite. After that time, he was able to redirect his desire to bite the doll rather than another child.

In order to monitor and prevent biting behavior, it is obvious that an adult must stay close to the child. Although this kind of supervision may seem like a lot of work, preventing biting will help a child to get through this problem without it escalating into a situation where victims are crying, parents are angry, and the child is being blamed for behavior that he cannot control without adult assistance.

If a child bites another child despite your attempts at prevention, try to have a consistent, calm response from all of the adults involved. Of course you must comfort the victim, who probably will be in tears. But at the same time, be aware that the biting toddler also may be upset by the reaction to his bite.

There are two appropriate types of responses to the child who has bitten. The first is to involve him in comforting the victim, soothing her and helping to apply ice to her wound. In this way, you are teaching and modeling empathy, for the children who are involved and for any other children in the group who are watching all of the action and learning from it. For some toddlers, this response is very effective. Other toddlers will not be able to help you with the victim, and your efforts to engage them will cause them to become resistant and defiant.

If a toddler who has bitten seems unable to pay attention to the victim, he probably is just caught up in his own confused feelings and needs. It can be very helpful to an upset or angry one-year-old to be separated from the group, preferably with an adult who can help him calm down. Once the child is calm, the adult can explain to him, "No biting. Biting hurts." It is no more helpful to bite a child yourself so that he will "know how it feels" than it would be to hit a child to teach him not to hit. However, if a child seems truly bewildered by another child's reaction to being bitten, you can let him know that it hurts by putting his own hand into his own mouth and letting him try biting himself.

If prevention and quick, calm responses do not work to eliminate biting behavior, or if the one-year-old who is biting also seems to be angry or unhappy, it's a good idea to look at other aspects of your child's life. Biting, like occasional nightmares, is part of the normal behavior of one-year-olds, but if the behavior seems to be unchanged or getting worse, your child may be experiencing some other stress that needs your attention.

33

CHOOSING CHILD
CARE FOR YOUR
ONE-YEAR-OLD

The majority of one-year-olds in this country have mothers who are employed outside the home. You already may have your child in the care of others, or you may be thinking about finding child care at some time this year. Like all parents, you want the best care for your child.

One-year-olds need almost as much attention as infants in order to thrive. Although a toddler has the ability to wait a few minutes to be fed or changed, she needs you to respond to her during almost all of her waking hours. Often, she just will need your attention for a moment, but if you tried to ignore her completely she probably would become more demanding and probably begin misbehaving. A one-year-old in child care needs the same constant attention, which means that one adult should not be expected to take care of more than four children who are less than two years old. (In family day care, one caregiver can take care of additional children *older than two* but not more than three babies and toddlers.) This is a minimum standard for the adult/child ratio, not an ideal, if you want your child to be attended to when she cries, or asks for milk, or wants a hug.

Equally important is that your one-year-old has consistent care from only one or two adults. In some child care programs, a group of children may be cared for by several adults who work together throughout the day, interacting with all of the children. This arrangement may be very practical for the adults, but a one-year-old needs the security of knowing that there is one person who truly cares about *her*. If she is cared for by a changing group of adults, no matter how kind they may be, she will become uncertain about who it is she should be trusting to take care of her while her parents are away. Many one-year-olds cope with this by becoming less attached to the adults who come and go, and playing by themselves throughout the day. Often, they don't seem upset at day care, but parents start to notice that they are becoming more easily upset and fearful about separation at other times. Fortunately, as more child care programs are being directed by individuals trained in early childhood development, the importance of having a "primary provider" assigned to each toddler is more widely recognized.

The child care setting you choose for your one-year-old should be safe. You should check every area for childproofing. Sometimes parents feel uncomfortable about inspecting other's households, but you may find that what seemed safe for one toddler is not safe for the others. A sitter will not know which child needs to have the gate hooked and which one shouldn't go down the stairs alone, so the whole house needs to be childproofed for the needs of the most reckless toddler.

Because one-year-olds are so physically active, they need space to run, climb, jump, and to ride and push wheeled toys. It's best to have outdoor space, but indoor space can be creatively arranged if this isn't possible. If there are parks nearby, a walk can be the highlight of every day.

Evaluating the basic needs of close adult supervision, safety, and space is just the beginning of finding quality care.

Your next step is to take the time to sit and observe the kind of activity and interaction that takes place between the caregivers and children in a program. There's no substitute for your own observations. It is your own instincts about people and your own understanding of your child that will help you decide if a setting "feels right" for you. Plan to spend an hour watching how the caregivers cope with children's demands, how organized they seem to be, the tone of voice they use, the general level of warmth and stability you sense. *Do not enroll your child in a day care program that will not let you observe!* Although instances of child abuse in day care are rare, they almost always occur in places where parents are restricted from visiting.

After you find a place that seems right for you, ask for names of parents to call for references. All responsible programs will be happy to give you names. Call at least three other families and ask them if they have any hesitation about recommending the day care to you.

Searching for care is hard work, especially if you have mixed feelings about leaving your one-year-old for long hours. You may want to choose the first place that seems reasonable, trusting that the caregiver has more experience with children than you do. You may want to choose a place with a glossy brochure and beautiful toys, feeling that a place that looks that good must be right. But it is the investment of your time in watching for what really happens to the children while they are being cared for that will pay off when you decide to leave your own child. You will know, because you have seen for yourself, that your child is being nurtured by someone who has a loving manner and a responsive personality, in a safe and stimulating environment. With this knowledge, your day at work will go much better.

HABITS

Habits are patterns that young children, older children, and even adults use for comfort, relaxation, and release of tension. Most habits are developed because they stem from basic instincts, such as the needs to suck, to be warm, to be held, or to express oneself. All children have many habits, ranging from cuddling a soft toy, to sucking on something, to twisting their hair or twiddling their fingers. As a parent watching your own one-year-old and her habits, you may wonder which habits are potentially problematic. In Keys 34–38 you will read about some of the most common habits of one-year-olds, why they occur, and some ways that you can respond to them effectively.

34

DRINKING FROM
A BOTTLE

Many one-year olds drink from a bottle. Parents often are told that their child should only be drinking from a cup by this age, but if their child seems attached to her bottle they wonder if it is necessary to take it away. Before you can decide what is right for your own child, you need to look at how your child uses the bottle. The major problem is not the bottle itself but the liquid in it.

A baby gets attached to bottles because she is born with a strong sucking instinct. As she learns that sucking liquid from the bottle nipple also tastes good and fills her stomach, she learns to associate the bottle with pleasant feelings. She starts to hold the bottle herself, and by the time she is a year old, she starts to think of the bottle as a security object, one that she can control with little assistance. The bottle also begins to be important as a symbol of comfort.

If a one-year-old still is using a bottle to drink milk or juice, there is a risk that this habit will damage her teeth. The child's primary teeth continue to appear this year (by the time she is two and a half, she'll have 20 teeth) and as they emerge, they need protection from decay. Every time a child sips from a bottle that contains anything but plain water, the natural bacteria in her mouth combine with the liquid to break down tooth enamel and start decay. A baby or toddler who falls asleep sucking on the bottle is at the biggest risk of damaging her teeth, because when she falls asleep she usually doesn't swallow the last few drops and they pool behind her teeth. These drops of milk or juice are slightly acid, and they rapidly break down the thin enamel of new teeth. If the toddler gets a cavity and does not have the cavity repaired the decay will continue to spread, eventually causing pain and putting her at risk for infection.

Some toddlers have the habit of having just one bottle of milk or juice in the morning and another one in the evening, draining each one rapidly. These children are not likely to get baby bottle cavities because the time that their teeth are being exposed to the liquid is so brief. Other children who have many bottles throughout the day or night, or fall asleep sucking on a bottle are more likely to have tooth damage.

The easiest way to change your child's habit is by gradually watering down her bottle without telling her. Begin by substituting one ounce of water for one ounce of the usual liquid. After two days, increase the amount of water to two ounces and reduce the amount of other liquid by another ounce. Continue to substitute another ounce of water every other day, and in just over two weeks, your child will be taking a bottle of plain water. Occasionally, a child will decide that she doesn't care for the replacement liquid and will stop using the bottle completely. Another child will decide that the pleasure she gets from the bottle continues no matter what the liquid inside it, but you won't have to worry about her harming her teeth.

Parents sometimes feel that if they take the bottle away completely, their child will refuse to drink milk. It is really much better to have a child who doesn't drink milk than one who has decayed teeth, and the majority of children eventually will learn to drink milk from a cup if they have no other choice. Don't flavor the milk in the cup to make it seem more attractive or you'll wind up with a new problem!

Once your child is taking a water bottle, you can decide if you want her to continue to use the bottle at all. Some children love to suck, and if they don't have a bottle they will suck their fingers instead. Other children feel attached to the bottle as if it were a favorite doll or blanket, and seem to get a sense of security from it. Still other children use the bottle as a way to calm themselves at the end of the day or as a ritual while they cuddle with a parent. If your child is using the bottle for any of these reasons, there is no reason to stop her. The use of the bottle is not psychologically harmful to the one-year-old and for many it is very beneficial. Bottles are a symbol of being a baby, and the one-year-old who is trying so hard to grow up may need this to feel comforted and safe.

If you don't want your toddler to have a bottle, you either can limit her use of it or get rid of it entirely. You might offer it only at certain times or to keep it at home. Most children will go along with these limits after a few days, but some parents may find it difficult to be firm, especially if one parent is more anti-bottle than the other. If you aren't successful at setting limits, it's better either to return to unlimited use of the bottle or to get rid of it entirely. Otherwise, the bottle will become part of an ongoing power struggle in your family and will be a source of frustration and comfort.

If you decide to get rid of the bottle completely, it's best to do so quickly. Choose a time when there are no other stresses or changes in her life. Because a one-year-old has no understanding of time, you don't need to prepare her much in advance. You can tell her one day that you are going to get rid of all of the bottles and that from now on she will drink from a cup. When she wakes up the next morning, tell her there are no more bottles. She may act sad or angry, but if you are calm and loving, she'll be fine. Plan to give her extra attention as she gets used to life without her bottle.

35

LOVEYS

Many one-year-olds become attached to a special object that they use to comfort themselves. These loveys sometimes are called transitional objects. They help a child transfer the warm, cozy feelings he experienced as a baby to an object that he can hold onto as he leaves babyhood and takes on the challenges of the big world. For this reason, your child may choose a lovey that he associates with the babylike sensations of sucking, smelling, or feeling a certain texture next to his face. Blankets, stuffed animals, or even sweaters can become the object of your child's affections and strong attachments.

Sometimes parents worry that if their child needs a lovey, it means that he is insecure. In fact, the child who can use a special object to settle himself and recapture feelings of security is showing great resourcefulness and strength. As a one-year-old begins to separate from his original source of security, his parents, he can boost his feelings of independence by carrying the substitute object with him. Some child development experts even suggest that parents try to introduce a security object to their child if he doesn't choose one on his own. If a parent holds a blanket or stuffed animal next to a child at bedtime and at special cuddle times the child may become interested, but this strategy often doesn't work. Some children never seem to need a lovey, and others are passionate in their attachment to one.

If your child has chosen a special object for comfort, respect his need for it. Think about getting a duplicate that you can rotate with the original so that one can be washed while the other is in use. The love object will be loved for its appearance, its feel, and its odor, so you may find that you have to work out a compromise between hygiene and familiarity! When a child loves a special blanket, parents sometimes will cut it in two parts, binding the raw edges, so that it doesn't wear out too fast. Some children can transfer the feeling for the big blanket to a small pocket size piece that they can take off to nursery school with them. Do make some rules about taking the lovey away from home. If your child gets in the habit of taking his special teddy bear everywhere, it's likely that the bear will be lost one day.

If your child has any kind of lovey, you may be tempted to give it to him every time you see him feeling sad or distressed. It's a better idea to let your child decide if he needs his comfort object, rather than you deciding for him. Sometimes a child needs to cry and have you comfort him, or be frustrated and calm himself. A lovey is just one way that a child learns to cope with his feeling, but it doesn't have to be the only way.

36

~~~~~~

BREASTFEEDING

The American Academy of Pediatrics and the U.S. Surgeon General recommend that all babies be breastfed until they are at least a year old. If you are breastfeeding your one-year-old, however, you know that most women don't continue breastfeeding nearly that long. The mother who chooses to nurse beyond a few months often hears comments such as "Are you *still* breastfeeding?" or "Aren't you ever going to stop?" Even if you enjoy nursing, you may have wondered if you should be thinking about weaning your child in the near future.

There is no reason to stop nursing your one-year-old until *you* feel that the time is right. Although breast milk alone will not meet your toddler's nutritional needs, the comfort and pleasure she gets from nursing can be wonderful. Most one-year-olds still have the need to suck, and continuing breastfeeding helps to satisfy that need. She also will get the closeness with you that helps to balance her need to assert her independence.

If you want to keep nursing your one-year-old, you'll need to feel confident in your choice in order to deal with negative reactions from other people. It may be easier to avoid situations where you can expect criticism or negative comments. You don't have to defend your decision unless you want to. Some women are able to deflect intrusive comments by saying nothing more than, "Thank you for your interest. I'll think about what you've said." If your partner is the one who is questioning your choice, you can talk about what it is about breastfeeding that is a problem for him. It may be that he is feeling left out of the relationship between you and your child or that he is concerned about "babying" your toddler. By hearing his point of view and looking at your child's developmental needs together, you should be able to work out a compromise that satisfies both of you.

Some one-year-olds may be nursing just a few times a day, but others like to nurse as often as they did when they were babies. Sometimes a mother feels as though she would like to keep nursing but not as often as her child demands. If this is the case for you, it's helpful to keep a record for a few days of your toddler's nursing patterns. You probably will find that there are times when your toddler seems to be getting a great deal of comfort from nursing and other times when she may be just touching base. You may find that you are offering to nurse when your child is distressed or unhappy. You also may notice that there are times when she asks to nurse when she seems to be bored or wants attention. Each of these requests for nursing can be met with a response other than breastfeeding, if you choose.

If you'd like to cut back on nursing, you can choose to nurse at certain times but not at others. For example, you could decide to nurse in the morning, at nap time, in the late afternoon, and at bedtime. At other times, you could distract your toddler with another activity or just tell her "Not now." You could decide to offer words and hugs rather than your breast, when your toddler is sad. Although it might be hard to set limits at first, most toddlers will adapt after a few days and the result probably will benefit your overall relationship with your child.

When you decide the time is right to stop breastfeeding, allow yourself several weeks to wean. Choose a time when you will not be going on vacation or having any new or stressful experiences. Begin by eliminating the feeding that you find least enjoyable or convenient. At that time, distract your toddler with an activity, a walk, a snack, or a hug. After two or three days, eliminate another feeding, using the same technique. Continue to eliminate feedings until your toddler is completely weaned. Be sure to give your baby lots of attention and cuddling in other ways and at other times. In this way, both of you will be eased through the change in your relationship.

Most mothers of nursing toddlers find that their breasts adjust easily to this slow weaning. If your breasts should get uncomfortably full, express a small amount of milk to relieve the pressure. If you express too much, you'll encourage continued milk production. After you stop breastfeeding completely, your breasts still will be able to produce a small amount of milk for several more months.

Once you wean your toddler, you probably will have some days of feeling sad about losing the tender relationship you shared. It's quite natural to feel this way. If you talk to other mothers, you'll find that these are feelings that occur every time a child takes a step towards growing up. Fortunately, the sad feelings that you have probably will be balanced within a few weeks by a realization that you feel more energetic than you've felt since your baby was born. Breastfeeding is valuable to mother and baby, but it is also hard work, and your body will feel the difference. Some women find that they need to watch what they eat very carefully or they gain weight. Others find that they had been carrying excess fat and fluid during nursing and that they suddenly lose five or ten pounds. Women vary so much in their patterns that you just will have to see for yourself how your body changes.

37

PACIFIERS

Many parents find that a pacifier is very comforting to their child, especially when she is an infant. Although some babies give up sucking a pacifier on their own, most will continue with a pacifier until their parents take it away. If you have a one-year-old who still is attached to her pacifier, it is extremely unlikely that she will give it up without your help, for two reasons.

The first reason is that a one-year-old still needs and enjoys sucking. If she did not suck on her pacifier, she might need to depend on a bottle, frequent nursings, or her thumb to satisfy this need. The second reason is that if your toddler has learned to associate sucking on her pacifier with getting comfort and pleasure, she may not know any other ways to get the same nice feelings. Parents themselves often use the pacifier as a way of helping an unhappy toddler to calm down, so the child feels that the pacifier, the parent, the comfort, and the sucking are all parts of what she needs to have when she is sad.

If your child uses a pacifier, there are probably many times when you are glad she does. You may have found that by sucking on a pacifier she can recover from frustration or fall asleep at night much more easily than if she had to do it on her own. You may feel that the pacifier is an important part of her life and see no need to modify her use of it at this time. If you feel this way, there is no reason to try to change this habit.

There are a few potential disadvantages to a toddler using a pacifier that parents should consider, although the disadvantages may not apply to your situation or may not outweigh the advantages for you or your child.

One disadvantage of pacifier use for a one-year-old is that a toddler cannot speak very well when she has a pacifier in her mouth. When she does, it usually is hard for others to understand her. Because a child develops her language skills by exchanging words with the people around her, a child who has difficulty speaking or getting responses from others might be delayed in learning to communicate.

Another disadvantage of pacifier use is that a child may become overly dependent on it for comfort. Some one-year-olds want a pacifier every time they get upset. For one child, that might mean just a few times a day. However, a very sensitive toddler might demand a pacifier every time she gets even slightly frustrated or angry. Because frustration and anger are common feelings for toddlers to have, some one-year-olds may become more and more dependent on the pacifier instead of learning other ways to deal with being distressed.

Sometimes parents are told that using a pacifier will damage a toddler's developing jaw or teeth. Fortunately, this common belief is not true. Although frequent sucking on a pacifier or a thumb can contribute to dental problems after age four, the one-year-old who uses a pacifier is not at greater risk for problems than the one-year-old who does not.

Before parents decide whether their one-year-old's use of a pacifier is a problem, it's a good idea to sort out whether the parents need the pacifier more than the child does. Sometimes parents have so much difficulty listening to their child cry that they rush to "plug her up" whenever she needs comfort. It's helpful for parents to think about their role in helping a child learn to manage unhappiness. If a child begins to feel that her crying is making her parents upset, she may start to believe that a pacifier or other object is a more reliable source of comfort than they are. A toddler needs to know that her parents are strong enough to stay calm even if she is out of control.

If you feel as though you would like to decrease or eliminate your one-year-old's use of a pacifier, you can begin by limiting the times when she is allowed to have it. Many parents find that it is relatively easy to begin by telling a child that from now on the pacifier stays at home. A next step, if you want to go further, can be limiting use of the pacifier to nap time and bedtime. (Some parents tell a toddler that she must keep the pacifier in her bed. This technique may work, but some resourceful toddlers will start going to bed every time they want the pacifier!) The final step would be telling your child that she is not going to be able to use a pacifier anymore, and taking the pacifier away for good. These steps should be taken only at a time when life is going smoothly for your child and your family, so that she is not under any extra stress that would be making her especially needy of her pacifier.

Most parents find that if they feel comfortable with the decision to lessen their one-year-old's use of the pacifier, their child adapts after a few days. If a child was primarily dependent on the pacifier for comfort, she usually will find another object to hold or snuggle if she needs one. If she was using the pacifier to satisfy her sucking needs as well, she may switch to sucking her fingers or her thumb. Of course, you won't be able to change this habit as easily as you can change the pacifier habit, so you may want to consider if you want to leave her pacifier use alone for now after all!

38

ᴀᴠᴠᴠ

ROCKING, HEAD BANGING, AND BREATH HOLDING

M any one-year-olds have habits that are not uncommon but are unusual enough to cause parents some concern. Most of the time these habits begin as a way for the child to comfort himself or to discharge feelings of tension. If the child persists in the habit, it may be a source of worry. Parents may be accepting of a habit when it begins, but then start to worry over time, "Is my child's behavior normal?" It is often helpful to talk to your health care provider about your child's habits, because someone who knows you and your child may be able to help you decide if a persistent habit is a problem. In this Key, you will learn about some habits that some children acquire.

Rocking. Most babies and toddlers use rhythmic movements to comfort themselves. Thumb sucking, ear pulling, and hair twisting are common behaviors. Other children have more elaborate habits, such as the toddler who rolled a button from his favorite sweater between his fingers while he sucked his thumb and cuddled in his mother's lap. All of these rhythmic habits probably stem from an infant's earliest memories of his mother's regular heartbeat and the comfort he received from being held close while he sucked. Some babies like to repeat and exaggerate these rhythms and like to be rocked. As they get older, they rock themselves, even to the point of getting on hands and knees to rock forcefully until they fall asleep. If a one-year-old continues this rocking habit, he may be strong enough to move his entire crib with his rocking. Some toddlers can rock hard enough so that their crib moves from one end of the room to another!

Although rocking can be a noisy and sometimes inconvenient habit, it usually is not a problem for the child. You may want to put a rug underneath the crib to keep it from moving. If your child seems to be unable to use any methods other than rocking to soothe himself, or if he seems to be tuning you out many times during the day while he rocks, talk to your health care provider about his behavior.

Head Banging. Some toddlers bang their heads against the side of the crib or on the floor in the same rhythmic way as the child who rocks. Generally, head banging is not a problem, because a toddler will stop when she hurts herself. Occasionally, however, a toddler will bang her head with so much force that she bruises herself. She may seem to be frustrated or even angry, and her parents can't soothe her. If this behavior is infrequent, your best response is to pad her crib or move her onto a soft rug when she feels the need to bang. If she continues to bang her head and continues to seem insensitive to pain, it is important to look at the rest of her life to see if she is under some stress. Is she getting overtired repeatedly? Is she not getting enough attention and soothing from adults? Is she being put in her crib for long periods when she is not ready to go to sleep? If you can't seem to find a way to control the banging or if it seems to be increasing in force and frequency, talk to your health care provider.

Breath Holding. When a toddler is having a tantrum, he may take in a deep breath to cry and then hold his breath. If he keeps holding his breath, his skin will begin to look gray or blue, and he even may pass out. As frightening as this may appear to parents, it is not a danger to the child. As soon as he has held his breath long enough to turn blue or go unconscious, his body's natural reflexes take over and he will begin breathing again. However, if parents panic and start to get upset every time their child begins to scream, fearing another breath holding episode, the toddler may get into the habit of breath holding every time he gets upset. Although repeated episodes are no more damaging than occasional ones, it's not a very easy habit to break. If your child has a breath holding episode and you are feeling anxious, talk to your health care provider about your worries. Breath holding, like any kind of tantrum behavior, is best managed by a parent staying casual and calm.

QUESTIONS AND ANSWERS

Our twenty-one-month-old says "ma," "da," and "ba," plus some other short sounds for different objects, but no real words. She is bright and loves to listen to stories, and she seems to understand everything we say. Should we take her to a hearing specialist?

If your child seems to understand you, and can follow directions without you having to point or gesture, she probably is hearing what you say. If she continues to add to her list of "labels," you can feel sure that she wants to talk, but just hasn't developed her ability to say words. Over the next few months, she should say more and more words. If she hasn't increased her vocabulary by her second birthday, talk to your pediatrician.

Our child was having nightmares when we returned from our family vacation and we brought him into our bed for several nights. Now he wakes up crying during the night and wants to come into our bed, but I don't think he's having a nightmare.

If you feel that your toddler is now over his fears and has developed a new sleeping habit, you can respond by going to him and telling him gently but firmly, "You're OK, go to sleep." You may need to return to his room several times to let him know that you haven't disappeared but that you expect him to fall asleep in his own room.

My daughter has two bottles of apple juice a day. She takes milk from a cup. How can I break her of the bottle habit?

Start to dilute the juice by adding one ounce of water to each bottle and subtracting an ounce of juice. Continue to add and subtract an ounce of water and juice every day until she is only taking water from the bottle. She may give up the bottle at this point. If she doesn't, she still may need to suck on something, and you will have to decide if you want her to have a bottle habit or another kind of sucking habit.

Why does our one-year-old throw food on the floor and how can we get her to stop?

Your daughter is throwing food on the floor because she enjoys throwing it more than she enjoys eating it. She may be letting you know that she is finished eating, or that you have put something on her plate that she doesn't like, or that you are giving her too much food at once. She also may enjoy the attention she gets from you for throwing food! If she just throws food occasionally, it's best to ignore her behavior. If it's a regular pattern, serve her small amounts of food at a time and watch for the signs that she's getting ready to throw. Tell her that if she throws food on the floor it means she's "all done" and that the meal is over. When she throws again, end the meal without scolding her or getting upset. After a few more days of testing, she won't throw her food unless she really is finished.

If my one-year-old falls down a lot should I be worried?

Most one-year-olds can't think as fast as they can walk and run, so they trip and fall often. Watch your child's pattern of falling. If he seems careless and clumsy, he's acting like most one-year-olds, but over the next few months his skills should improve.

147

Does my one-year-old need extra fiber in his diet?

If your child is eating fruits and vegetables and whole grains, he probably is getting enough fiber. Even if he doesn't care for these foods, you don't need to worry as long as his bowel movements are soft and formed. If he has hard or painful bowel movements, talk to your health care provider about any need to change his diet.

My one-year-old is on the go from morning to night. He runs and climbs and can't sit still. Is he hyperactive?

Most one-year-olds are very active and some are also very active by temperament. It's not a good idea to label a child as hyperactive this young. Try to structure his day so that he has many opportunities to play actively and see if that helps to direct his energy. Don't expect him to sit still for more than five minutes, and try to choose quiet activities that are interesting to him to help him build his attention span.

My husband and I don't agree about discipline. We have different family backgrounds and beliefs. How can we work out our differences?

If two parents are in disagreement about how to manage a toddler's behavior, it's likely that they will continue to disagree as the child gets older. It would be much better for your child if you could read some books, talk to other parents, or take some parenting classes together to help you bridge the gap between your beliefs.

When I take my toddler to her play group she wants to sit in my lap almost all morning. Eventually she'll play with other children, but usually it's time to go home by then. What can I do?

Your child may be the sort of person who takes a long time to feel comfortable in a new situation. As she sits in your lap, she has time to observe the other children and get used to being there. If you try to push her, she may cling to you more. Try arriving at the play group early, so that she can be settled before the other children arrive.

I know that one-year-olds have tantrums, but my son's screams could shatter glass! How can I get him to stop screaming so loud?

You can't. Your son's screaming is just an intense way of protesting. It's best to ignore his screaming, just as you would ignore any kind of tantrum. If you try to get him to be quieter, he will learn that by screaming he gets attention. He might learn to scream even louder.

GLOSSARY

Cognitive the mental process of learning and understanding.

Constipation hard or dry bowel movements. Infrequent or irregular soft bowel movements are normal and are not signs of constipation.

Development the act of growing or expanding. In children, development occurs both gradually and in spurts. Development can be physical, cognitive, or emotional.

Nightmare a dream that causes a child to wake up tearful or afraid and usually in need of comfort.

Night terror a partial arousal from sleep that causes the child to thrash about, scream, or cry. The child is calm as soon as he is fully awake and does not seem afraid.

Oppositional behavior combative or contrary responses to parents from children. The behavior typically is seen in one-year-olds who are learning to be independent.

Sleep association habit the pattern that an individual follows to fall asleep at bedtime and after arousals from sleep during the night. Some children and adults are very inflexible in the way in which they can fall asleep; others are more adaptable.

Temperament the inborn behavioral style that influences the way a child interacts with his caregivers and the environment.

Time out a method of interrupting a child's misbehavior by separating him from his activity for a brief period.

SUGGESTED READING
AND RESOURCES

Balaban, Nancy. *Learning to Say Goodbye: Starting School and Other Early Childhood Separations*. New York: New American Library, 1987.

Brazelton, T. Berry. *Toddlers and Parents*. New York: Dell Publishing Co., 1989.

Chess, Stella and Thomas, Alexander. *Know Your Child*. New York: Basic Books, 1987.

Ferber, Richard. *Solve Your Child's Sleep Problems*. New York: Simon and Schuster, Inc., 1985.

Satter, Ellyn. *Child of Mine: Feeding with Love and Good Sense*. Palo Alto, California: Bull Publishing Co., 1986.

Child Help: National Child Abuse Hot Line (24-hour resource and referral for parents under stress): 1-800-422-4453.

INDEX

DR. BALTER'S STEPPING STONE STORIES

Dr. Lawrence Balter,
Illustrations by Roz Schanzer

Each of the storybooks in this series deals with a particular concern a young child might have about growing up. Each book features the same cast of characters—the kids who live in the fictional town of Crescent Canyon, a group to whom any youngster can relate. The stories are thoroughly entertaining while they help kids to understand their own feelings and the feelings of others. Engaging full-color illustrations fill every page! (Ages 3–7) Each book: Hardcover, $5.95, 40 pp., 8" x 8"

A Funeral for Whiskers:
Understanding Death ISBN: 6153-5

A.J.'s Mom Gets a New Job:
Adjusting to a Separation ISBN: 6151-9

Alfred Goes to the Hospital: Understanding a Medical Emergency ISBN: 6150-0

Linda Saves the Day:
Understanding Fear ISBN: 6117-9

Sue Lee's New Neighborhood:
Adjusting to a New Home ISBN: 6116-0

Sue Lee Starts School:
Adjusting to School ISBN: 6152-7

The Wedding: Adjusting to a
Parent's Remarriage ISBN: 6118-7

What's the Matter With A.J.?:
Understanding Jealousy ISBN: 6119-5

ISBN PREFIX: 0-8120

Books may be purchased at your bookstore, or by mail from Barron's. Enclose check or money order for total amount plus sales tax where applicable and 10% for postage and handling (minimum charge $1.75, Canada $2.00). Prices are subject to change without notice.

Barron's Educational Series, Inc.
250 Wireless Boulevard
Hauppauge, NY 11788
Call toll-free: 1-800-645-3476

IN CANADA:
Georgetown Book Warehouse
34 Armstrong Avenue
Georgetown, Ontario L7G 4R9
Call toll-free: 1-800-247-7160